The Sting and the Twinkle

THE
STING
AND THE
TWINKLE

Conversations with Sean O'Casey

edited by

E. H. MIKHAIL
and
JOHN O'RIORDAN

BARNES & NOBLE

BOOKS

10 East 53d St., New York 10022
(a division of Harper & Row Publishers, Inc.)

First published in the United Kingdom 1974 by
THE MACMILLAN PRESS LTD

Published in the U.S.A. 1974 by
HARPER & ROW PUBLISHERS, INC.
BARNES & NOBLE IMPORT DIVISION

ISBN 06-494818-8

Printed in Great Britain

To Eileen
whom O'Casey called
'the pulse of my heart'

Contents

CONTENTS   ix

Acknowledgements

This book appears by kind permission of Mrs Eileen O'Casey, to whom we are deeply indebted. We are especially grateful to her and members of her family for their ever-helpful advice and encouragement, and for permission to quote from some of Sean O'Casey's letters, previously unpublished.

The anthology owes its original idea to Professor Edward Mikhail, whose *Sean O'Casey: A Bibliography of Criticism* (London: Macmillan; and University of Washington Press, 1972) served as a basis for its compilation.

The compilers offer their sincere thanks to those authors and interviewers, publishers and editors of journals whose names are mentioned below or in the footnotes to the individual contributions, and whose kindness and co-operation have made this selection possible. In particular, our thanks are due to the National Broadcasting Company of America for permission to include parts of the televised filmed interview, 'A Conversation between Sean O'Casey and Robert Emmett Ginna'; to the New York Public Library, in particular Mr James W. Henderson, Head of the Research Libraries, and Mrs Lola L. Szladits, Curator, Berg Collection, for allowing us to quote portions of the transcript contained in the Berg Collection of their manuscripts, and to Robert D. Graff and Robert Ginna for permission to include some of the transcript; to the BBC for allowing us to use the transcript of the discussion programme, 'Playwright and Box Office', as printed in the *Listener*; to Plough Productions Ltd, of Dublin, for permission to use the passage on p. 95 from the filmed documentary, 'Cradle of Genius: A Tribute to the Abbey Theatre', to Paul Rotha, Tom Hayes and Jim O'Connor, in the same connection, and especially to Mrs D. Brignull, of Southgate Technical College, London, for making a transcript of the hilarious dialogue; to Hugh Webster for the use of extracts on p. 116 from a Canadian Broadcasting Corporation programme, to Mr Robin Woods of the Program Archives Department for help in tracing details of this, and to Mrs Mary Sharp for making a transcript for our use; and to Jean M. Smith, of Southgate, for her valued assistance in translating the Russian text of Boris Izakov's interview.

Acknowledgements not fully covered in the footnotes for permission to reproduce copyright material are due to Associated Newspapers Group

Ltd (article from *Daily News*), David Higham Associates ('Sean O'Casey; or A Rough Diamond'), the International Herald Tribune Corporation (article from *New York Herald Tribune*), the Abbey Theatre: the National Society Ltd ('Au Revoir to the Abbey Theatre'), the Irish Press Ltd ('O'Casey and the Critic'), the *Morning Star* (article from *Daily Worker*), and to the copyright-holders of the following: *Joseph Holloway's Abbey Theatre: A Selection from his Unpublished Journal 'Impressions of a Dublin Playgoer'*, ed. Robert Hogan and Michael O'Neill, Copyright © 1967 by Southern Illinois University Press; *The Movies, Mr. Griffith and Me*, Copyright © 1969 by Lillian Gish and Ann Pinchot (by permission of W. H. Allen & Co. Ltd and Prentice-Hall, Inc., Englewood Cliffs, New Jersey); Gjon Mili, 'Tea and Memories and Songs at a Last Fond Visit', *Life* Magazine, Copyright © 1964 by Time Inc.; Harold Clurman, 'O'Casey: For All his Curses, A Yea-Sayer', *New York Times*, Copyright © 1969 by the New York Times Company; and Bosley Crowther, 'Who is Then the Gentleman?', *New York Times*, Copyright © 1934 by the New York Times Company.

The publishers have made every effort to trace the copyright-holders, but if they have inadvertently overlooked any they will be pleased to make the necessary arrangement at the first opportunity.

For assistance and information generously given, we wish to thank: Dr Ronald Ayling, Allan Chappelow, Miss Carol Coulter, Rupert Croft-Cooke, Michael J. Durkan, Robert Johns, Professor David Krause, Eric Partridge, David Phethean, Don Taylor, and J. C. Trewin.

Special words of thanks to Tim Farmiloe of Macmillan for his enthusiasm and encouragement and to Harry Bawden of the same firm for his help in seeing the book through the press. We are grateful to Mr Oliver Stallybrass for compiling the index.

E. H. MIKHAIL
JOHN O'RIORDAN

Introduction

I

Up till the present, interest has centred largely on Sean O'Casey's plays and other writings. Even now, there is no definitive biography, spanning the whole of his life. Considering the picturesque public image he presents—

> the Aran sweater; the unlighted pipe tucked in the corner of a broad and firm mouth the thick-lensed glasses perched bravely on the bridge of a notable nose; the skull cap with some few wisps of white hair escaping from under it [1]

—his comparative biographical neglect seems, at first, somewhat surprising. Little is known, however, of O'Casey's early life before he was knocking at the door of the temple of Dublin's Abbey Theatre in the nineteen-twenties, save what he tells us—in a phantasmagoric way ('weaving a pattern', he styled it)—in such early autobiographical works as *I Knock at the Door* and *Pictures in the Hallway*.

His wife's recent endearing portrait, affectionately titled *Sean*—published in 1971—is a touchingly intimate portrayal, honest and heartfelt in its approach, and gives a side to his character never before fully appreciated: O'Casey intensely happy in his new-found surroundings, in his marriage, his children and a whole new world of books and pictures and music. It does not touch, of course, on the forty-seven years of the playwright's eventful life before his marriage, in London, in 1927. *Sean O'Casey: The Man I Knew* (1965), by Gabriel Fallon, is informative on O'Casey's emergent years as a playwright, though there is no reference in such a memoir to the dramatist's early life while working in successive labouring jobs in working-class Dublin. Professor David Krause, who wrote a satisfying study —mainly from a literary standpoint—*Sean O'Casey: The Man and his Work* (1960)—is preparing for publication the Collected Letters;

1. Robert Hogan, Introduction, *Feathers From The Green Crow* (1962), p. ix.

and, when these are eventually published, a very significant personal dimension of O'Casey's life will have been revealed.

To help fill a gap in the present biographical coverage, the following interviews and recollections—dating mostly from 1925 (when Sean O'Casey was scaling the heights of his theatrical career) until the time of his death in 1964—have been brought together as an anthology by the present editors, in the hope that scholars, admirers and the general reader will discover for themselves a playwright of Promethean qualities, with an unquenchably comic spirit and, clearly, out of sympathy—though by no means out of touch—with his contemporaries, both in the drama and the immediate artistic world around him; a brave, forthright personality—at once beguiling and stimulating, with a passionate concern for the whole of humanity; a man who, throughout the eighty-four years of his life, was noted for his complete integrity.

The title of this anthology derives from one of the interviews contained in this collection, and suggests, in symbolic form, O'Casey's own bitter-sweet nature: waspish in some directions, dove-like in others. The contumeliousness among Irish authors is well known. Harold Macmillan once remarked, 'I don't attempt to keep pace with the quarrels of my Irish authors. They are bosom friends when I meet them on one occasion; a few months later the same people are deadly enemies. I keep outside it all.' [2]

The Sting and the Twinkle is, therefore, another seasoned helping of O'Casey cornucopia, and, as in most of his writings and plays, the tragi-comic muse is much in evidence throughout. Pungent and provocative, the anthology is in the same lively tradition as its predecessors. *The Flying Wasp* (1937), *The Green Crow* (1956), *Under a Colored Cap* (1963), and *Blasts and Benedictions*, issued posthumously in 1967.

II

Most of the interviews comprising this collection contain firsthand records of conversations with Sean O'Casey. Almost all have appeared previously in the form of newspapers, journals and books—mainly in British and American publications. In some instances, to avoid duplication of similar topics, a condensed version of the original is given in the interests of continuity and readability.

2. Monk Gibbon, *The Masterpiece and the Man: Yeats as I knew him* (London, 1959), p. 167.

O'Casey, like Shaw, detested interviews and press ballyhoo of any kind, but the richer and rarer occasions when he allowed himself to be in the spotlight were the gala events in a meteoric career, as on the eve of a major production of a new play or the launching of a special festival of a group of his best-known plays. At such times, he was often in hilarious mood, and would sometimes regale his astonished interlocutor with a rousing, 'roysterin'' song! (His stage characters are endowed with the same sonorous accomplishments; they break into song when the audience least imagines.)

His interviewers come from all walks—from established authors, professional critics, actors, theatre directors and producers, to photographers from the film world, journalists, university students, casual acquaintances, as well as, of course, lifelong friends.

The interviews, which are arranged chronologically, cover a wide range of topics: biographical descriptions of the playwright's appearance and temperament; his own idiosyncratic pronunciation of English; his occasional hoaxing of interviewers, whom he once referred to as 'the lordly ones' (those 'precious ponderers with frightened minds and souls'); details of important places in his career; references to his earnings, his eye-trouble and his constant battle with ill-health; his serio-comic outlook on life—his opinions about Communism, Christianity, Russia, England, Education, Universities, and the Atom Bomb. His attitude towards Ireland; and how he kept in touch with Irish life while resident in England. His opinions concerning the Abbey Theatre; Irish actors and Irish writers His views on Yeats, Joyce, Lady Gregory and Shaw— belonging, like O'Casey himself, to 'the indomitable Irishry'. His comments on the English Theatre, municipal theatres, and the National Theatre: as well as his comments on his own writings, the descriptions of his methods of work, his earliest experiments as a playwright, the sources of some of his plots and characters, his preferences among his own plays, his references to particular productions: the development of his style, and authors who influenced him: his views on television as a medium for his plays.

III

The majority of interviews in this collection offer their own brand of O'Casey wisdom and humour. In addition, we are able to supplement these impressions with the observations of others who knew the dramatist equally well, as recorded elsewhere. What were the views of these contemporaries?

The Irish actor, Jack MacGowran, who played in major roles in some of the later publications, has stated [3] 'O'Casey's pen was deceptive. From his writings many people thought him narrow and bitter, but he was the antithesis of these things. He wrote with rage about narrow institutions because he himself was broad in mind, and he wrote with an acid pen because he disagreed with so many establishments. He was a wonderfully expansive man to talk to, full of good humour. Within half an hour of your meeting him, he would want to sing ballads. He wanted to create joy and be surrounded by joy. He used his plays as a platform for this belief and never gave up until the end of his days.'

Desmond Ryan, the Irish historian, has written [4] 'there was a force and character about him even if you thought he was a crank, a fanatic, a man whose mind had room for only one idea at a time. In private he had a courtesy and simplicity.' 'He was a very amusing person and the best company you could possibly ask for,' said Denis Johnston.[5] 'O'Casey held the centre of the stage as he was entitled to do. He was a very good mimic, acting out the stories he told you. He was really Joxer Daly.' 'I knew Sean O'Casey and liked him very much,' said Tyrone Guthrie;[6] 'I don't think he was the most reasonable of people, but he had more than compensating qualities of heart and mind.' 'A disgruntled fellow,' wrote Thomas Clarke, one of the leaders of the 1916 Rising.[7] 'Terrifically argumentative. A bit like Shaw,' was the opinion of a neighbour—a Torquay nurseryman.[8] 'He is a great man,' Lawrence of Arabia wrote in a letter to Lady Astor, dated 15 February, 1934, after seeing the London performance of *Within the Gates*; 'I have learned a great deal from him. . . . When a rare Irishman does go on growing, he surpasses most men. Alas that they are so rare.' [9] Bernard Shaw, after he had finished reading *The Silver Tassie*, O'Casey's great anti-war play, referred to its author, in one breath, as a 'Titan', and in the next, 'You really

3. Des Hickey and Gus Smith, *A Paler Shade of Green* (London, 1972), p. 104.
4. *Remembering Sion* (London, 1934), p. 84.
5. *A Paler Shade of Green*, p. 62.
6. *Ibid.*, p. 111.
7. *Feathers From The Green Crow*, Introduction, p. x.
8. Eileen O'Casey, *Sean* (London, 1971), p. 242.
9. *The Letters of T. E. Lawrence*, ed. David Garnett (London, 1938), p. 790.

are a ruthless ironfisted blaster and blighter of your species'![10]
Augustus John, in one of his autobiographical sketches, contents
himself by saying, 'I could swallow any quantity of O'Casey's
superb fun, and ask for more. Thank you great-hearted Sean!' [11]

Alluding to himself, in *Blasts and Benedictions*, O'Casey says 'I
am what is called a shy fellow, dreading to meet a new acquaintance,
but, invariably, if the newcomer be anyway human I make friends
in a few minutes.' And Joseph Holloway, the inveterate chronicler
of first nights at the Abbey, noted down in his Diary, after attending
the first performance in 1923 of *The Shadow of a Gunman*, '. . . quiet-
mannered almost to shyness, and very interesting in his views.' [12]
'The most gentle of men,' wrote W. R. Rodgers in his obituary.[13]

IV

Nearly all the interviews in this collection took place after O'Casey
had exiled himself for good from Dublin. Some were written while
he was in London and New York (he spent several weeks in America
to launch his most ambitious play, *Within the Gates*), but by far the
majority were obtained with O'Casey's permission while the playwright was living out his last, contented years in Devon, which had
become for him a second Ireland—Devon being, he tells us, 'almost
all a Keltic County, founded by a Keltic tribe, which gave its name
to the county, a tribe that came over long before the gallant Gaels
came sailing over the sea to Eirinn.' [14] Although he had left Ireland,
he was, as he relates in *Inishfallen, Fare Thee Well*, 'no more of an
exile in another land than he was in his own'. Why did he leave
Ireland? Among the many reasons he gave at first was the one he
told the newspapers at the time:

> I have a good deal of courage, but not much patience, and it takes
> both courage and patience to live in Ireland. The Irish have no
> time for those that don't agree with their ideas, and I have no
> time for those who don't agree with mine. So we decided to
> compromise, and I am coming here. The English are more tolerant
> and they believe a lot.

10. *Sean*, p. 85.
11. *Finishing Touches* (London, 1964), p. 50.
12. *Joseph Holloway's Abbey Theatre*, ed. Robert Hogan and Michael J.
O'Neill (Southern Illinois Univ. Press, 1967), p. 216.
13. *The Sunday Times* (London), 20 September, 1964, p. 15.
14. *Sunset and Evening Star* (1954), p. 91.

Later, as O'Casey discovered, the English became indifferent and ignored a dramatic genius on their doorstep. O'Casey, in his plays, didn't go out of his way to praise England or Ireland, for that matter, though he wasn't anti-English as Orwell and Agate supposed; nor was he really anti-Irish, either. Although he was savage in his criticisms of Irish clerical humbug and British political chicanery, he had a warm affection for friends in both countries, and many of his most ardent correspondents were long and respected friends living in America, Russia and elsewhere. Only a few years before he died, he said in a letter to an Irish friend,

> With all good wishes to The Little Dark Rose: [15] may she widen her roots, strengthen her stem, add to her foliage, and bloom fresh and strong in the coming times.

O'Casey's cynicism towards Ireland was that of a man who loved his country but who wanted it to be more to his heart's desire.

Ironically, O'Casey, who shunned interviews whilst in the full glare of the dramatic limelight, was never free of publicity and interview-seekers for the remainder of his life, hidden, though he was, deep in Devon. Those interviewers who won his esteem have given, on the whole, remarkable close-ups and perfect cameos of a fighting personality, who was fierce in his beliefs for the future progress of mankind and yet who was overflowing with kindness for those whom he admired and loved. Some of these interviewers, at times—possibly with tongue in cheek—adhered to the belief that there were moments when it seemed as if the principal characteristic of the interviewee was deliberately to take the opposite view of what was expressed by the person he was talking to! This, however, was only a surface impression, because the interviewer soon came under the spell of the vibrant personality and would be carried away by the sheer vehemence of his thoughts. He would cease to be greatly concerned with the rightness or wrongness of O'Casey's opinions, and simply enjoyed listening to a good conversationalist. To hear Sean O'Casey confessing he couldn't stand Chesterton or Auden or the Weary-Willie poets and Tired-Tim playwrights of today was far more refreshing and entertaining than listening to a formal talk about such a subject on radio or television. O'Casey, the lovable eccentric, was always completely interesting in mind and character, even in his apparent wrong-headedness.

15. Ireland.

Although almost blind in his final years, the skull-capped figure still peered out at the rest of the world with an auspicious eye: auspicious for youth and hope, beauty and sentiment—indeed, anything likely to add to the gaiety and happiness of the nations; reserving the lash of his scorn for official pomp and everyday complacency, tilting a Quixotic lance at those authors, playwrights and critics who were brave in the pursuit of their own timidity. 'Let the timid tiptoe through the way where the paler blossoms grow; my feet shall be where the redder roses grow, though they bear long thorns, sharp and piercing, thick among them!' says Ayamonn, who represents much of his creator, in that searchingly autobiographical play, *Red Roses for Me*.

Like many a superlative Irishman, there was more than 'a dint o' wondher'—as one of his own characters remarks—in his conversation, which was truly laced with 'a gold embroidery o' dancin' words'. His talk was excitingly like the dialogue of his own plays and writings, and could be compared to his own description of the poetry, which he greatly loved, of Hugh MacDiarmid: 'it tore along like flood through a gorge, bubble, foam, and spray flying from the deep rushing stream'.

V

It may seem a curious contradiction that although Sean O'Casey avoided publicity, discouraging many a prospective interviewer from visiting him, he often allowed himself to be 'interviewed' by post, from sometimes altogether total strangers, many of whom were young, enthusiastic, admiring, American students. One such—a fourteen-year-old student from Jacksonville, Florida, Susan Brown —had written to him, in his eighty-fourth year, cheekily asking him to name the book which had made a lasting impression on him, which, in his opinion, would be 'just too good for a teen-ager to miss'. His reply is the reply of an affectionate, wise-hearted elder statesman, intensely concerned with the problems of the young (the fifth volume of his autobiography, *Rose and Crown*, carries the dedication 'To the Young of All Lands, All Colours, All Creeds'):

What book influenced me most and what is my favourite book? Two big questions, Susy, two big questions. So big that I can't get around them—I don't know. I love hundreds and hundreds, those many I was able to buy I like well, and those I wasn't able to buy I like better.

Throughout my life, however, my favorite books that have influenced me most are books that aren't books at all. Now what d'ye make of that? Think a minute; well? They are two—my eyes and my ears, Susan. We haven't to pay for these, nor have we to borrow them from a library. They are born in our bodies and we carry them with us everywhere we go. We must take care of them, of course, and we must use them. Many having them never do; they go about like the heathen idols who have ears and hear not, eyes but they see not, so they use them only to keep from knocking into things. Your ears let you hear music, song of bird, hum of bee and they let you know what others are saying. Your eyes let you see the faces of mother and father, the lovely faces of flowers, the colors of a bird's plumage, the sparkle of a river, the loveliness of a sky, and the stars therein. These are books indeed!

As for your class's choice of the bible as 'the best book', crowds have chosen it over the centuries as a sacred book, containing all knowledge necessary to salvation—all presumably christians. Well, my dear, I don't know what the word 'salvation' means, so must leave that choice to itself. I like the book for its beautiful, simple, and flexible English, its lovely rhythmic prose but I seek my philosophy, my science, my history of man in the accumulated knowledge gathered by men and women through the years and proved by trial.

As for a book of my choice containing everything lovely and meant to be enjoyed, that has no class or creed, that promises nothing except loveliness, I choose the Works of Shakespeare; his plays, poems, and sonnets ...

Another teen-age student from Brooklyn—Judy Goldberg—in the last year of his life, had written, requesting his answers to some challenging questions ('Naughty girl to put such a terrible Challenge before my poor frightened face!'), including 'What qualifications do you feel are necessary for a person to fulfil himself as a playwright?' and 'What challenges have you faced in your career as associated with the theater?' Never taken aback, he replied:

You ask what qualities should one have to be a playwright: As many as possible, Judy—an education formal or acquired; a fine knowledge of the language you speak, of your country; as wide a knowledge of literature as your mind can hold; knowledge of another language; a keen eye that can see things others are blind to, and a keen ear to hear a phrase originally comic or pathetic; and a fine memory to remember all you hear worth hearing, and all you see which is worth seeing. As well, a love and knowledge of nature outside of our own humanity, tree, shrub, plant, river, hill, and valley; the flowers that grow in them, or bloom along streams and ornament the hedgerows; insects, ugly and beautiful, and that wonderful spinner of silk, the spider. Shakespeare knew them all. Of course, knowledge and love of these things is enjoyable and makes us fuller men and women, even though we never gave a thought to playwriting. They are a vital part of man's life. I would never advise anyone to aim at becoming a professional playwright; the road from a play's first conception to the stage is a long, long trail, often full of false hope, disappointments, anxious days, maybe years, and in the end rejection. We meet all these throubles, of course, in any kind of life; and my last advice to you is to be brave facing all of them. Courage is the greatest of virtues. 'Compassion for another's sorrow, courage in your own'.

He himself was faithful to his own ideals. His letter to Lady Gregory, on the eve of the rejection of his play, *The Silver Tassie*, by the Abbey Theatre, in 1928, was a call to courage.[16]

. . . You can always walk with your head up. And remember you had to fight against your birth into position and comfort, as others had to fight against their birth into hardship and poverty, and it is as difficult to come out of one as it is to come out of the other, so that power may be gained to bring fountains and waters out of the hard rocks.

He was a man of outstanding courage, himself, particularly when one considers his handicap of partial blindness and the fact that he raised himself up from poverty to world renown. He had to fight hard to emerge from illiteracy, from life in the slums of his native Dublin, from the sweat and tear of jobs that would probably have destroyed the spirit of a lesser man. Above all, he had to face the vehement disapproval of his countrymen and poverty or near-poverty for many years, even after he was married and living in England, especially during and after the second world war. He was often close

16. *Journals, 1916–1930* (London, 1946), p. 105.

to what he called 'the snarling snout' of want. Yet he, himself, was never afraid of odds.

He triumphed over it all, and in the process wrote a group of masterpieces that are one of the chief glories of the theatre of the world. After his first Dublin plays, he was, as J. C. Trewin has suggested,[17] ahead of his time. His conversations, too, like his maturer plays and essayistic writings, are full of provocative and soul-searching maxims, expressed as always in that enchanting, celtic incandescent prose which never failed to capture the hearts of his listeners and audiences. Just as in his flamboyant comedy, *Cock-a-Doodle Dandy*, or his final collection of essays, entitled, significantly, *Under a Colored Cap*, his conversations are extraordinary dialogues of combative discussions of orthodox beliefs and the myths and mysteries that have perpetuated them. Gaiety, freedom and intrepidity were ideals he cherished, and these he defended throughout his own long life, vigorously and relentlessly. He remained, to the end, an incorrigible rebel, but a colourful one.

JOHN O'RIORDAN

17. Introduction, *Sean*, p. 13.

London, N.14
1974

Interviews and
Recollections

Portrait of O'Casey as a Young Man*

R. M. FOX†

The Sean O'Casey whom I met in Dublin in the early 'twenties, was a slightly-built man with piercing eyes, a sensitive mouth and the mobile features of an artist. This was about a year before his first play, *The Shadow of a Gunman*, was staged at the Abbey, in 1923.

We met in the upper room of Delia Larkin's flat in Mountjoy Square. Delia was the sister of the herculean, eloquent Labour agitator, Jim Larkin, for whom O'Casey and myself shared a common enthusiasm. Larkin was imprisoned in America, a victim of an earlier witch hunt on McCarthy lines. I had written an article calling attention to his case. This was published in a Scottish journal and I sent a copy to Delia.

* * *

Staying in Dublin on my vacation from Ruskin College I came to know O'Casey well and found him friendly, unassuming and helpful. He asked me what I would do when I left Oxford. I told him I was coming to Dublin to write.

'I have known scores of people who left Dublin to write,' he said, 'but I have never known anyone coming here for that purpose.'

Not many years later he joined the Irish literary exiles.

In those days he was managing a little social club run by Delia Larkin for which he received the sum of £1 a week. He had done some writing, including a strike play [1] for Liberty Hall [2] in 1913, the

---

* Extracted from *Irish Times* (Dublin), 1 December, 1964, p. 8. Expanded version of an earlier article, 'Sean O'Casey's Dublin', *Irish Times*, 2 May, 1960, p. 8.

† Irish historian. Author of *Green Banners: The Story of the Irish Struggle* (London, 1938) and other works.

1. *The Harvest Festival*—one of O'Casey's earliest plays, rejected by the Abbey Theatre. This and other apparently lost apprentice works are discussed in *Feathers From The Green Crow*, pp. 269–72.

2. Trade Union headquarters in Dublin.

year of industrial turmoil. But he had never done any professional writing for the theatre. Later, when I was writing for the *Irish Statesman*, I spoke to the Editor, George Russell (A.E.) [3] about his work. He said that O'Casey had submitted many plays to the Abbey but they could not be done as they were full of 'propaganda'.

*   *   *

On the eve of the Civil War, O'Casey took me round Dublin. We went to the Fowler Hall in Parnell Square, the headquarters of the Orange Lodge in the city. This building had been seized by the Republicans and was being used—with Irish irony—to house Belfast refugees who had fled from the northern city. A big tricolour flag in green, white and gold, billowed from an upper window.

'I know the Commandant here,' said O'Casey. 'You will find it interesting and useful if you are writing.'

He knocked at the door. As we stood on the step a burly, red-faced farmer came along the street.

O'Casey parleyed through the letter-box and the heavy door was unbarred. There were chains across and we could just squeeze through. Sandbags stretched across the hall and a man was lying there with a rifle. We stepped over and went upstairs.

*   *   *

In a large upper room the refugees were housed. They were roughly curtained off with blankets. Heaps of bedding were dotted along the room. Here were old people and children from the North. But what fascinated me were the huge paintings hanging round the room. There were portraits of Queen Victoria, Lord Carson [4] and other Orange worthies in official robes, gazing down in glassy disapproval.

I heard the stories of the refugees. Then O'Casey told me that if I wanted to write about the place, the Commandant wanted to see what I wrote first.

'What for?' I demanded, bristling at the idea of censorship. 'How can these pitiful stories injure the garrison here?'

'That's all very well,' said O'Casey, 'but as well as the refugees

---

3. Poet and essayist, contemporary of Yeats.
4. Ulster Unionist leader, who was opposed to Home Rule and who founded the Ulster Volunteers to fight against British forces to ensure that Ulster would remain part of Britain.

on the top floor, they have a store of ammunition in the basement! They were expecting attack at any moment. That's why we were so long in getting in.'

*   *   *

When we had finished at the Fowler Hall, O'Casey took me to another building where a Sinn Fein[5] Court was in progress, a crowded room where cases were being tried. This assembly was illegal under British law but even Tory lawyers were attending and pleading because the official courts were deserted.

*   *   *

Such scenes as these formed the seed bed of O'Casey's material and helped to foster his dramatic genius. When he wrote *The Shadow of a Gunman* he used living characters whom I knew well.

*   *   *

In the early years—before the Rising of 1916—O'Casey, as Secretary of the Irish Citizen Army,[6] wrote militant—even military— articles in *The Irish Worker*.[7] He urged that people should arm if it were only with hurley sticks or ancient halberds. But when the fighting came his sensitive spirit reacted to the suffering of the old, the infirm, the poor—the most defenceless victims of the struggle.

This feeling inspired his greatest play *Juno and the Paycock* and gave to Juno her finest speech. The dramatist of the Dublin tenements had his material all round him.[8] And, although he was over forty before he was able to get expression, he has left an imperishable heritage to the world.

5. Political arm of the I.R.A., favouring an independent, all-Ireland republic.
6. An army for the Irish Workers, formed in 1913, the year of the great industrial strike, to protect them from police attack.
7. *Feathers From The Green Crow*, pp. 21–31, 44–55.
8. 'He was a true voice of the Dublin underworld, as he gazed from the tenement doorways, with their broken fanlights and dilapidated stairs,' wrote R. M. Fox, later, in the chapter entitled 'Civil War and Peace', in Sean McCann (ed.) *The World of Sean O'Casey* (London, 1966), p. 49. 'The people, too, in O'Casey's vision, had that fierce flame of individuality which burned through sorry circumstances and held hope of redemption.'

Discovering Sean O'Casey*

LADY GREGORY †

15 April, 1923. At the Abbey I found an armed guard; there has been one ever since the theatres were threatened if they kept open. And in the Green-room [1] I found one of them giving finishing touches to the costume of Tony Quinn, who is a Black-and-Tan [2] in the play, and showing him how to hold his revolver. *The Shadow of a Gunman* (Sean O'Casey's first play) [3] was an immense success, beautifully acted, all the political points taken up with delight by a big audience. Sean O'Casey, the author, only saw it from the side wings the first night but had to appear to make his bow. I brought him into the stalls the other two nights and have had some talk with him.

Last night there was an immense audience, the largest, I think, since the first night of *Blanco Posnet*. Many, to my grief, had to be turned away from the door. Two seats had been kept for Yeats and me, but I put Casey in one of them and sat in the orchestra for the first act, and put Yeats in the orchestra for the second. I had brought Casey round to the door before the play to share my joy in seeing the crowd surging in (Dermod O'Brien caught in the queue), and he introduced me to two officers, one a Colonel. (Yeats had wanted me to go with them to a *ball* given by the army, 'good names being wanted'!)

Casey told me he is a labourer, and, as we talked of masons, said he had 'carried the hod'. He said, 'I was among books as a child, but I was sixteen before I learned to read or write. My father loved books, he had a big library. I remember the look of the books high up on shelves.'

* *Lady Gregory's Journals: 1916–1930*, edited by Lennox Robinson (London: Putnam, 1946; New York: Macmillan, 1947), pp. 71–3, 74–5.

† Co-founder, with W. B. Yeats, in 1904, of the Irish National Theatre Society. For many years, a Director of the Abbey Theatre. Author and playwright (1852–1932). Her book, *Our Irish Theatre* (1913; repr. Gerrards Cross: Smythe, 1972), describes her early work in this field. She was called by Shaw 'the greatest living Irishwoman'; and O'Casey, whose veneration and friendship she won, spoke of her as 'Blessed Bridget o' Coole'.

1. The recreation room for the company and players.
2. Auxiliaries supplied by the British in 1920 during the Anglo-Irish conflict.
3. The first night was on 12 April, 1923.

I asked why his father had not taught him and he said, 'He died when I was three years old [4] through those same books. There was a little ladder in the room to get to the shelves, and one day when he was standing on it, it broke and he fell and was killed.'

I said, 'I often go up the ladder in our library at home,' and he begged me to be careful.

He is learning what he can about art, has bought books on Whistler and Raphael, and takes *The Studio*. All this was as we watched the crowd.

I forget how I came to mention the Bible, and he asked 'Do you like it?' I said, 'Yes. I read it constantly, even for the beauty of the language.' He said he admires that beauty, he was brought up as a Protestant but has lost belief in religious forms. Then, in talking of our war here, we came to Plato's *Republic*, his dream city, whether on earth or in heaven not far away from the city of God. And then we went in to the play. He says he sent us a play four years ago, *The Frost in the Flower*, and it was returned, but marked, 'not far from being a good play.' He has sent others, and says how grateful he was to me because when we had to refuse the Labour one, *The Crimson in the Tri-colour*, I had said, 'I believe there is something in you and your strong point is characterization.' And I had wanted to pull that play together and put it on to give him experience, but Yeats was down on it. Perrin says he offered him a pass sometimes when he happened to come in, but he refused and said, 'No one ought to come into the Abbey Theatre without paying for it.' He said, 'All the thought in Ireland for years past has come through the Abbey. You have no idea what an education it has been to the country.' That, and the fine audience on this our last week, put me in great spirits.

*   *   *

8 March, 1924. In the evening to the Abbey with W. B. Yeats, *Juno and the Paycock* (Sean O'Casey's) [5]—a long queue at the door, the theatre crowded, many turned away, so it will be run on next week. A wonderful and terrible play of futility, of irony, humour, tragedy. When I went round to the Green-room I saw Casey and had a little talk with him. He is very happy.

4. This was a miscalculation of his age; he was six when his father died. Until he was about 45, he admitted, he hadn't a notion of when he was born. His birth certificate establishes the date as 30 March, 1880.

5. The first performance was on 3 March, 1924. Barry Fitzgerald played the role of 'Captain' Boyle, Sara Allgood 'Juno', and F. J. McCormick 'Joxer' Daly.

I asked him to come to tea after the next day, the matinée, as I had brought up a barmbrack for the players, but he said, 'No. I can't come. I'll be at work till the afternoon and I'm working with cement, and that takes such a long time to get off.'

'But after that?'

'Then I have to cook my dinner. I have but one room and I cook for myself since my mother died.'

He is, of course, happy at the great success of his play, and I said, 'You must feel now that we were right in not putting on that first one you sent in—*The Crimson in the Tri-colour*. I was inclined to put it on because some of it was so good and I thought you might learn by seeing it on the stage, though some was very poor, but Mr Yeats was firm.'

He said, 'You were right not to put it on. I can't read it myself now. But I will tell you that it was a bitter disappointment for I had not only thought at the time it was the best thing I had written but I thought that no one in the world had ever written anything so fine.'

Then he said, 'You had it typed for me, and I don't know how you could have read it as I sent it in with the bad writing and the poor paper. But at that time it was hard for me to afford even the paper it was written on.'

And he said, 'I owe a great deal to you and Mr Yeats and Mr Robinson, but to you above all. You gave me encouragement. And it was you who said to me upstairs in the office—I could show you the very spot where you stood—"Mr Casey, your gift is characteriza-tion." And so I threw over my theories and worked at characters and this is the result.'

Yeats hadn't seen the play before, and thought it very fine, remind-ing him of Tolstoi. He said when he talked of the imperfect first play, 'Casey was bad in writing of the vices of the rich, which he knows nothing about, but he thoroughly understands the vices of the poor.' But that full house, the packed pit and gallery, the fine play, the call of the Mother for the putting away of hatred, made me say to Yeats, 'This is one of the evenings at the Abbey that makes me glad to have been born.'

O'Casey in Dublin*

JOSEPH HOLLOWAY †

28 March, 1924. A bitterly sharp evening with an icy cutting wind about. I had a long chat with O'Casey in the vestibule of the Abbey. He thinks the Government [1] is proving a set of woeful incompetents —egotistical and intolerant of criticism. They are going from bad to worse. They'll be nobody's friend shortly. He spoke of the hypocrisy over the shooting of the soldier at Cork. 'The honour of Ireland is at stake over it, people say who don't know what honour is!'

He witnessed terrible deeds during recent years; a friend of his was riddled with bullets and mutilated in a horrible way by the Green and Tans, a young Tipperary lad. Nothing could be more brutal than the treatment he got. It is hard to think Irish people capable of such savagery. Savages would be decent in comparison to them. After the inquest his remains were brought to his digs, and O'Casey helped to carry in the coffin to his friend's upstairs. Another lad he knew was taken out and tied up by his hands—his feet dangling some distance from the ground, while they poured salts through a tin dish down his throat. . . . The poor fellow was cut down alive, but he is a human wreck ever since—always shaking, though as brave as ever. . . .

15 April, 1924. . . . O'Casey, speaking of the English and Irish, said, 'Although I write cynically about the Irish in my plays, I have a much greater opinion of their intellects than I have of the English. I understand English politics, but I never met an Englishman who understood the Irishman's outlook.' [2]

* *Joseph Holloway's Abbey Theatre: A Selection from his Unpublished Journal 'Impressions of a Dublin Playgoer',* ed. Robert Hogan and Michael J. O'Neill (Carbondale and Edwardsville: Southern Illinois University Press, 1967), pp. 228, 230, 232, 235–6, 247.

† Bachelor-Architect of the Abbey Theatre, who saw practically every great actor and every interesting play that appeared in Dublin during his adult lifetime. (He died in 1944, aged 83.) Holloway's journal, comprising over 200 semi-legible notebooks and stored in the National Library of Ireland, serves as a reminder of the excitements of those early Abbey years.

1. The Irish Free State Government.

2. Denis Johnston, *Collected Plays* (1960), in his introduction to his play, *The Scythe and the Sunset,* tells us: 'When Sean O'Casey first came to live in

20 May, 1924. At Webb's[3] I came across Sean O'Casey. . . .
O'Casey is amused when he hears people say, who never were in a
tenement, that his plays are photographic of the life he depicts. They
not knowing anything at first hand of what they are talking. . . .

On his telling me he had purchased a volume of AE's collected
poems,[4] I mentioned that he would be writing his next play amongst
the stars. Then he told me of the play with the title of *The Plough
Amongst the Stars* (*sic*) he had in his mind to write. He also got two
volumes of Nietzsche at Webb's. . . . He regretted the loss of several
books he lent, such as McGill's *The Rat Pit*, a very realistic book.
He thinks James Stephens's *The Charwoman's Daughter* a very
pleasingly written story, but scarcely true to slum life.[5]

*   *   *

14 August, 1924. . . . I witnessed a strange incident last night in
seeing W. B. Yeats and Mrs Yeats being crowded out of the Abbey,
and having to seek the pictures to allay their disappointment.
O'Casey's play, *The Shadow of a Gunman*, had been staged for three
nights with the usual result—that crowds had to be turned away
each performance. This and his other play, *Juno and the Paycock*,
have wonderful drawing power. The same people want to see them
over and over again. . . . And the author stood chatting to me in the
vestibule the other night as the audience came thronging in, proud of
the fact, but in no way swell-headed, his cloth cap cocked over his
left eye, as his right looked short-sightedly at the audience's eager
rush. Certainly he has written the two most popular plays ever seen
at the Abbey, and they both are backgrounded by the terrible times
we have just passed through, but his characters are so true to life and
humorous that all swallow the bitter pill of fact that underlies both
pieces. The acting in both reaches the highest watermark of Abbey
acting. . . .

12 November, 1925. 'If I were left about £2000, I'd never work

---

London in the 'twenties, he was strap-hanging one late afternoon in a crowded
Tube train; and, after contemplating for some time the unbroken vista of open
newspapers, bowler hats, rolled umbrellas and shopping bags, he was finally
heard to remark, "*Look at them—all burning with indignation over the Irish
question!*" '
3. Famous book shop in Dublin.
4. Soaked in mysticism.
5. Stephens, like O'Casey, was reared in the slums of Dublin and brought up
in poverty with practically no schooling.

again,' said Sean O'Casey to Mr Cummins and me in the vestibule of the Abbey during Act II of *Androcles and the Lion*. 'Want has been the terror of my life,' he added, and went on to say that 'When I was earning 19/8 a week, I was always in dread of being out of a job. I never drank and paid for lodgings and food out of my wages and played football, having joined a Gaelic Club [6] for recreation. When out of work I used to live on a cup of tea at morning and night, and all my little things went in pawn even to keep body and soul together.' He thinks he is naturally lazy and wouldn't work if he had means of support; his ideal of pleasure would be to sit by a river and laze away in chat with anyone. . . .

O'Casey would go to London for the first night of his play, *Juno and the Paycock*, on Monday, 16th November next. . . . He has settled up the contract with Fagan [7] over the London season and hopes the play may have a long run. . . .

6. The St Lawrence O'Toole Club.
7. J. B. Fagan—Manager of the Irish Players who presented O'Casey's plays to London audiences, 1925–6. He finally managed to coax O'Casey over for the production, as later interviews reveal, in March 1926.

The Author of *Juno*: An Informal Talk*

I knocked at a door in the hall of a high tenement house in Dublin.[1]

A man in his shirt-sleeves answered. The man was Sean O'Casey, whose play, *Juno and the Paycock*, has come to the Royalty Theatre, London.[2]

As he finished dressing in the darkness of the room where he lives, works, and sleeps, cooking for himself as he did when a bricksetter's labourer, two years ago, he talked in his soft Dublin tongue, using the speech of a writer and the accent of a workman. 'Born in a tene-

* *The Observer* (London), 22 November, 1925, p. 9. Despite the anonymity of the interviewer, it is apparent from a subsequent interview, contained in this collection—'O'Casey in Buckinghamshire'—that the interviewer here is J. L. Hodson.

1. 422 North Circular Road.   2. It opened on 16 November, 1925.

ment house, I write about people in tenement houses,' he told me.
'If the London production is a success, I'll leave 'em for ever.'

*   *   *

Mr O'Casey is forty-four, is frank, unaffected, likeable, and (so he
says) lazy. A slim, hatchet-faced man, with pointed nose and chin,
and brown, twinkling eyes, so weak, I believe, that he has to hold his
manuscript six inches or so from his nose to read what he has written.
He works at all hours when the mood and the idea are there. 'I make
no divisions of day and night,' he said. He writes in copybooks,
leaving the play loose and flexible, and then types it out twice, altering, altering. 'It would not be true, perhaps, to say that the first draft
bears no resemblance to the finished play, but they are very different.'

I spoke to him of technique. 'I abominate it,' he said. 'They tell
me *The Shadow of a Gunman* (his first accepted play) breaks all the
rules. If the characters live and the play holds the audience, that's
enough.'

*   *   *

Mr O'Casey has had a hard life. He told me his father died when
he was six, and that his mother brought the family up. 'We had dry
bread and a drink of tea in the morning, and that again at night if
we were lucky.' For nine years he half-starved. At fourteen he taught
himself to read: at fifteen, he worked for a newsagent from 4 a.m.
to 7 p.m. for 9s. a week. After that he navvied and laboured for fifteen
years. His last job, oddly enough, was on a building near the Abbey
Theatre, which he has visited for the past ten years and into which
he drops nearly every evening.

*   *   *

He has views on education. 'Education is a terrible drawback to a
dramatist—I mean the sort of primary and secondary education we
get in Ireland. You can see from the way my plays are written I never
went to school.' He said that quite seriously. 'The first book I bought
was Shakespeare. I spent nearly all my money on books.'

I mentioned the criticism that has been made that his plays are a
series of photographs, that he writes only of what he knows, of his
own experiences. 'What in the name of Heaven should a man write
about?' he asked. 'What did Euripides and Aristophanes write
about? My next play will be *The Red Lily*—about a prostitute. I

wonder if that will suit them? I worked with Captain Boyle, a character in *Juno*, for five years. I didn't even alter his name. No, I don't
think he ever saw the play.'

On the subject of acting he said he had acted a little in an amateur
way. 'But I go to all the rehearsals in the Abbey, and I sometimes act
the characters for them there.'

Mr O'Casey wrote at least three plays—one two-act and two three-
act—before *The Shadow of the Gunman* was accepted in 1923. Since
then he has written *Cathleen Listens In* (a topical extravaganza on
the current political scene in Ireland), *Juno and the Paycock*,
Nannie's Night Out (one-act), and *The Plough and the Stars*, which
he has just completed. Lady Gregory, Mr Yeats, and Mr Lennox
Robinson think highly of *The Plough*,[3] he told me. It will be done
at the Abbey Theatre soon.[4] 'The output isn't bad,' said Mr O'Casey,
'but I'm afraid I'm very lazy.' Of the future, he declared, 'One
never knows what one will write, but I'll never write a novel. I don't
like novels. But plays! I think writing plays, bringing people to life
—that is charming work. I wouldn't change that for anything.'

3. Described by Lady Gregory, *Journals*, p. 98, as 'an overpowering play'.
4. 8 February, 1926.

How a Tenement Dweller
Studied the Stage*

Sean O'Casey, the remarkable Irish playwright, who until six weeks
ago was a labourer, has arrived in London for the first time in his life.

He has never before crossed the Irish Channel, and he has come
here expressly to see his play, *Juno and the Paycock*, when it is trans-
ferred from the Royalty to the Fortune on Monday, March 8th.

'My first impression of London has been one of sleeplessness,'[1] he
told a newspaper representative. 'Everything was so quiet last night
that I listened for the familiar noises of the tenement quarter in which

* Shortened version of the interview, entitled 'Sean O'Casey Sees London:
Irish Dramatist's First Visit to England', which was published in the *Evening
Standard* (London), 5 March, 1926, p. 4.

1. Cf. Holloway's *Journal*, Saturday, 6 March, 1926, p. 267.

I live in Dublin. An author should live in the atmosphere of the places and people about whom he writes. Then only can he hope to get a true perspective.

'Thus I wrote about people of tenement regions, and I lived, and still live, in a single room in a quarter like to that I have tried to describe.

'Whatever literary attainments I have came from a desire for knowledge. The trouble with our modern system is, as it seems to me, that we study too much. Education suffers from too much study. What is more important is a true perception of the relation of learning (a hateful word) with art and literature.

'Modern civilisation must learn that all intelligence does not belong to the middle or upper classes. The working classes have their share, and I think the time will come when everybody, son of a cook, son of a millionaire, will go to the same schools.

'In my life I regret nothing, not even the hardship of manual work by day and the endeavour to keep awake to teach myself to read and write at night. In Dublin there is a blessed institution—a book barrow. When I was young I used to save my twopences and threepences, and go down to buy school books. In my little attic I learned grammar, and I knew that a noun was the name of a place or a person, but it took me weeks to master the adjective, for I could not understand what it meant to qualify a noun.

'In those days my vocabulary was only disyllabic. The first serious book I ever bought was a shilling copy of the Globe edition of Shakespeare, and I learnt *Hamlet*, *Macbeth* and *Julius Caesar* by heart.

'But reading Shakespeare did not make me a playwright. It happened in this way: I was a member of a Gaelic or national club, which had for its original object the teaching of Irish and the encouragement of the hurley game. One day they decided to produce a play, but because they had no money the plays they tackled were very uninteresting.

'By this time I could write a little, and I was presumptuous enough to suggest that I wrote a play myself.

*   *   *

'When *The Shadow of a Gunman* was produced at last by the Abbey in 1923, I was elated, and began to write phantasies on politics. One of these, *Cathleen Listens In*, was done at the Abbey,[2] but it was

2. First performed on 1 October, 1923.

so badly received that I went home almost broken-hearted, without going behind even to thank the artists. And that same night in my attic I sat down to write *Juno and the Paycock*, and here I am in London fulfilling an ambition.'

Too Shy to See his Own Play: Sean O'Casey's First Night in London*

A thousand people sat in a West-End theatre last night alternately laughing and weeping, while the man whose genius swayed their emotions sat alone in a neighbouring hotel, too shy to make his London début.

The man was Sean O'Casey, bricklayer's labourer, train hand and dramatist; the play was *Juno and the Paycock*, which provided the dramatic sensation of 1925.

I found Mr O'Casey, a man in the forties, Irish of feature, silver-grey hair over his temples, eyes heavy-lidded. He was in a mood of humorous introspection.

'I've come to the wrong side of the Channel for the first time in my life because they talk of doing *The Plough and the Stars* soon.[1] They think it's a great play, but in Dublin some of them thought it was a slur on the Irish nation. It's all about the Irish civilian army in 1916, the name comes from their flag. It's a better play than *Juno*.[2]

* *Daily Graphic* (London), 6 March, 1926, p. 2.

1. Had its London premiere at the Fortune Theatre in May 1926.
2. Holloway's *Journal* records: 'There was electricity in the air before and behind the curtain at the Abbey Theatre when *The Plough and the Stars* was first produced.' [Monday, 8 February, 1926.] His entry for Thursday, 11 February states: 'A great protest was made to-night, and ended in almost the second act being played in dumb show . . . to-night's protest has made a second *Playboy* of *The Plough*, and Yeats was in his element. . . . Some of the players behaved with uncommon roughness to some ladies who got on the stage, and threw two of them into the stalls. . . . The chairs of the orchestra were thrown on the stage, and the music on the piano fluttered, and some four or five tried to pull down half of the drop curtain, and another caught hold of one side of the railing in the scene in Act 3.'

'Yes, it's all true I was starving, many a time I was. . . . *Juno* I thought out while I was walking about the scaffolding of a new building.

'Oh, yes, I have lots of ideas for new plays. I want to write one called *The Signal*, about the railway; one called *The Red Lily*, about a fallen woman; another on a Catholic's religious doubts. I want it to be called *The Cock Crows*.[3]

* * *

'I feel I'll never do as Barrie has done and come and live in England. A dramatist, I think, can make a single spot symbolical of the whole world. Hardy does it, Chekhov does it, Balzac does it. They're translating *Juno* into Scandinavian and German, by the way.

'I don't fancy I'll like London. Where's your penny trams to take you into the country? I live in the slums of Dublin; oh, haven't you ever been in Dublin? At sunset, as you stand on the quays and look around at the blue mountains. . . .'

Mr O'Casey is going to take his first real look at London to-day.[4]

To-morrow night at 5 o'clock he will broadcast on the London wavelength (2LO) a talk on 'Irish Plays'.

3. Although he never wrote plays with such titles, the ideas were inherent in some of his later plays—e.g. *Within the Gates, Cock-a-Doodle Dandy*, and *The Moon Shines on Kylenamoe*.

4. His impressions of London, after a five-week visit, were published in the *Daily News* (London), 24 May, 1926, under the title, 'London Passes By', and reprinted in *Blasts and Benedictions* (1967), pp. 237-40.

Dramatist who was On the Dole*

Sean O'Casey the Irishman who climbed suddenly from the ranks of starving out-of-works to the pinnacle of a successful dramatist, has arrived in London in connection with the production of his *Juno and the Paycock*, at the Fortune Theatre, on Monday, March 8th.

To an interviewer, he spoke openly of his early privations:

* *Daily Herald* (London), 6 March, 1926, p. 1, originally entitled ' "Dole" Dramatist: Out-of-work Irishman's Climb to Fame'.

'I have been three times on the dole, and the devil a much I got out of it either,' he said. 'When I was pounding the Abbey Theatre, in Dublin, with manuscript, I fell into a queue each day to draw 2s. 6d.[1]

'I was working at nearly all kinds of jobs, even road making. But from the human beings I worked with I got the life I have since put into my work.

'I was on strike with them. I starved with them, and I looked for jobs with them.'

He explained that his first efforts at play writing were due to his association with the O'Toole National Club, whose activities 'were hurling, football and amateur theatricals'.

1. O'Casey had submitted three plays that were rejected by the Abbey before *The Shadow of a Gunman* was finally accepted—*The Frost in the Flower*; *The Harvest Festival*; *The Crimson in the Tri-colour*.

'Paycock' in London*

I had a chat with Sean O'Casey in a quiet café yesterday with Mr and Mrs J. B. Fagan.

A slight, almost insignificant-looking man until one catches his small penetrating eyes, he has no false estimation of his position as an artist or man of the world, and until we talked of the miserable wages of the labourer he was complacent as a dove.

'Three weeks before *Juno and the Paycock* was produced,' he said, 'I pawned my trousers for five shillings and earned wages insufficient for the nourishment of a dog.

'What's the use of singing "The Red Flag" when men will accept 30s. for a week's hard labour?'

*   *   *

Incidentally Sean O'Casey said he thought his next play [1] would wreck the Abbey Theatre.

Talking of English playwrights, he said they did not appeal to him. Galsworthy had enormous power and conviction, but his style

* *Daily Sketch* (London), 6 March, 1926, p. 5, originally entitled, 'Sean O'Casey Talks'.

1. *The Silver Tassie*, published 1928.

was, perhaps, a little too polished and in danger of being untrue to life.

'The Irishman,' he went on, 'hasn't any sentimentality. He behaves when he is drunk as an Englishman does when he is sentimental.'

*   *   *

While we talked someone walked in and nearly roused O'Casey to anger.

'I suppose,' he said, 'that when you have made a lot of money you'll move among the best people in Dublin.'

O'Casey blew a cloud of smoke.

'Tell me,' he replied, 'do your best people live in tiled bathrooms or floorless barns?

'I shall continue to live in my room where I have always worked,' he concluded. 'There is a fine fellowship with those among whom I lived minus a shirt for months.'

*   *   *

'I like London, but I don't understand the English. What did that waitress say? The bill? That should have been obvious enough.'

Fame at Last*

It is not every successful playwright who has found it necessary to pawn his trousers. That distinction belongs to Mr Sean O'Casey, whose Irish play, *Juno and the Paycock*, is having so successful a run in London at the Royalty Theatre.

A fortnight before its production in London Mr O'Casey, who was then in Dublin, was reduced to about a shilling.

'So I took my best pair of trousers along to the pawnshop,' he told a reporter yesterday. 'They were a very good pair. They cost 35s., and I was sorry to part with them.

' "I want 10s.," said I, as I put them on the counter.

' "Five shillings," said he. And that's all I got for them.' [1]

---

* *Daily News* (London), 6 March, 1926, p. 5, originally entitled 'Playwright's Last Shilling'.

1. See, also, Lady Gregory's *Journals*, p. 256.

'Do you mind,' asked the newspaper representative, 'if I mention that?'

'Not a bit,' said Mr O'Casey, with a smile. 'There's nothing to be ashamed of in pawning your trousers.'

Things have changed for him since then. But success has by no means turned his head. He is still the same quiet, cautious, humorous man that he was in the days, only a short time ago, when he earned a bare living as a bricklayer.

He drifted into writing plays through his experience as an amateur actor. He came to the conclusion that he could write better plays than those in which he took part, and, after a few attempts, he leapt into fame with *Juno and the Paycock*.

When asked what he thought of London, he replied: 'I've seen some very pretty girls here—very pretty indeed.'

'Perhaps you'll marry a London girl?'

'I don't know that—but I might think about it,' he said characteristically.[2]

2. He married Eileen Carey Reynolds—the Irish-born actress brought up in England—the following year in London.

London at his Feet*

Sean O'Casey spent the week-end quietly wandering about London with his fellow-countryman and colleague James Bernard Fagan. There is material for a first-class film drama in O'Casey, the ex-bricklayer's labourer, making his first visit to the London which he has conquered with a single play.[1]

'Have you any idea of emulating Barrie and Shaw and making money by poking fun at us Londoners?' I asked him.

'No. I think I shall live in Dublin. And I don't like Barrie's plays,' he replied. 'They're too pretty, and life isn't pretty.' Nobody who has lived in Ireland since 1916 could very well think it was. Besides, O'Casey was once walking about the streets of Dublin starving.

* *Daily Graphic* (London), 8 March, 1926, p. 5.

1. Nearly 40 years later, in 1965, Metro-Goldwyn-Mayer made a film of O'Casey's early life story, entitled *Young Cassidy*.

S.T.—2*

Still, the world should be a nicer place for him now. By the end of
the year, *Juno and the Paycock* will have been played in five different
countries, and his royalties in each are a good deal fatter than the 50s.
a week of the Abbey Theatre, Dublin.

From Starvation to Success*

CONSTANCE VAUGHAN †

I began badly—as though interviewing came not as naturally to a
journalist as honey-gathering to a bee. And it was not so much that
this was the Dublin labourer, the much-lauded tenement-dweller
who has proved a second Synge, and is at the moment the prey of
London lion-hunters. That might happen to anyone.

But this was the man whose *Juno and the Paycock* had proved
fine enough to lead Mr George Bernard Shaw, most wise, most impatient of critics, to the box-office twice. Knowing which I could
only question lamely: 'Er, er, how did you start?' and Sean O'Casey
in his pleasant, almost inaudible way [1]—a sort of brogued mutter—
replied:

'Oi started as a baby; a very weak baby; a very irritable baby; and
a very hungry baby. And Oi remained a very hungry choild.

* *Daily Sketch* (London), 24 March, 1926, p. 7, originally entitled 'O'Casey
Explains Himself'.
O'Casey won the Hawthornden Prize, in 1926, for his play, *Juno and the
Paycock*, as the best work of imaginative literature—prose or verse—published
during the year. This Prize was instituted in 1919. The 1926 Selection Com-
mittee consisted of Miss Alice Warrender, Laurence Binyon, Robert Lynd,
Edward Marsh and J. C. Squire. The Earl of Oxford presented the award to
the author at the Æolian Hall, London, on 23 March, 1926 (*The Times*, 24
March, 1926, p. 11). 'It was with the greatest difficulty,' said J. B. Fagan to a
news reporter afterwards, 'that we managed to get O'Casey to come over to
England at all. He refused the Hawthornden once because it entailed his
attendance in London. When, however, the authorities waived that rule, he
came.' (*Daily Graphic*, 24 March, p. 5.) Lady Gregory recalls that O'Casey
asked her whether he should accept the award, as he had refused to send a
copy of *Juno* for the competition or inspection. She said, 'Certainly, it is a
compliment and the £100 will buy a good many new trousers.' (*Journals*,
p. 256). See previous interview, 'Fame At Last'.
† Journalist; mainly connected with the *Daily Sketch*.

1. Cf. Desmond Ryan, *Remembering Sion* (London, 1934), p. 81: 'Half to
himself he speaks, lowering his voice to an intense whisper.'

'And still as a very hungry choild, Oi got my first job as errand boy to an ironmonger at 4s. a week. You see, my father died when Oi was about six years old, and so my elder brothers, who had all been fed and educated, came off better than Oi did.

'And now Oi suppose you'll be wanting to hear what Oi was doing after that. Working, sleeping, eating, drinking, cursing, starving, fighting, courting, going on strike, reading, educating myself in my leisure moments, and learning the Oirish language.

'Or was it perhaps how Oi started playwriting that you were after knowing? Oi started by accident. Oi had joined a sort of club in Dublin, where they taught you Oirish, and dancing, and all that, and we used to act and produce plays. Awful plays.

'So one day Oi said: "Oi'll write you a play worth acting." So Oi sat down and wrote *The Frost in the Flower* (good toitle, isn't it? Oi like good toitles for me plays!). But the committee wouldn't have it. It wasn't good enough.

'But it was, and Oi knew it was, and so Oi sent it up to the Abbey Theatre. They sent it back with a letter, a kind letter, beginning, "Almost a good play, but not quite," pointing me out the faults. Oi wrote two more, but each one the Abbey sent me back. So Oi burned them [2] and wrote my first success, *The Shadow of a Gunman*.

'Oi was working as a labourer at the time; and everyone was pleased at the success Oi had got. Then came *Juno and the Paycock* and *The Plough and the Stars*.

'Yet Oi had never really loiked the drama. Oi loathed it. Oi loiked the theatre. Oi remember long ago, when the great Irving came to Dublin for a week, Oi went to see every performance he gave. Oi was then an odd man, a smith's helper, and my whole week's salary went on seeing Irving, and it was worth it, too!

'After my first success Oi bought myself a typewriter to help me after Oi'd written my stuff. No, Oi do *naat* wroite straight on to the machine. It comes to me hard and Oi write slow.

'Sometimes Oi wish Oi was a labourer again—it's a grand loife for a man—a grand loife. It gives me almost a homesickness to pass men now knocking down houses and building roads.

'For you can't sever yourself from humanity, for there's nothing else that counts. Didn't Synge say, "Although his head may be in the stars his roots must be in the earth"?

2. *The Harvest Festival*, alone, has survived. The manuscript was acquired by the New York Public Library for its Berg Collection, in 1969.

'And that's my oidea of Art. There must be blood in all things that are written, in all pictures that are painted, in all songs that are sung. There must be the cry of humanity; it may be a ferocious cry, a bitter cry, an angry cry; but if it isn't a human cry it isn't Art. For loife is the primary fact.

'Yes, Oi like London and Oi like the English people Oi have met very, very much indade. But Oi couldn't live here, and Oi'm going back to Dublin soon to work.

'Oi'm publishing my play over here, *The Plough and the Stars*, and Oi'm dedicating it to my mother. My mother had a wonderful laugh, a beautiful laugh, and Oi heard her laugh a quarter of an hour before she died. And Oi am dedicating my play *"To the Gay Laugh of my Mother at the Gate of the Grave."*

'Someone from the newspapers here came to interview me (O'Casey's eyes were ironic), and they asked me, "When you go back to Dublin, now that you're successful, will you live among the best people?"

'So will you tell them, please, for they seem to be under a mis-apprehension about me, that Oi have *always* lived among the best people?

'And Oi have chosen them myself. Oi have always had as my friends Billy Shakespeare and Goya and Balzac, and Anatole France and Shelley, and many another.

'But, of course, Oi don't know who you may be calling your Best People over here!'

Sean O'Casey: A Worker Dramatist*

R. M. FOX †

It was at Easter in 1922 that I first met Sean O'Casey, just on the eve of the last tragic struggle in Ireland. He went with me to the Fowler Hall—the Orange headquarters in Dublin—which had been seized

* Extracted from *New Statesman* (London), 26 (10 April, 1926), pp. 805-6.
† See note on p. 13.

by Republicans and was being used to house Belfast refugees. . . .
We parleyed a little and a stranger came up. He was a fresh-coloured,
plump farmer from the country. He had a worried look.

'Where are you from?' asked O'Casey.

'From Cork,' was the answer.

'And how are things down there?'

'Bad, very bad!' said the Cork man, shaking his head dolefully.
'Both sides are handing out arms to everyone. Why can't they agree
to differ?'

'Agree to differ, there's a thing to say,' said O'Casey. 'How can
people agree to differ? If they agree, they agree; if they differ, they
differ!'

'Yes,' said the Cork man. 'But what I mean is that the army should
not dominate the people.'

'Oh, that!' said O'Casey, 'that's easily solved. Let the people join
the army. In a properly constituted State the people are the army!'

The look in his eyes showed that he did not intend to be taken too
seriously. Incidentally, he was applying the *reductio ad absurdum*
to militarism. His plays are full of similar whimsicalities.

Sean O'Casey's experiences in the toiling underworld of Dublin,
and the grinding oppressive weight of life under these circumstances,
acting on a man of his temperament, have helped to create that
powerful surge of feeling which is present in his plays. It is working-
class drama—stark, slum drama. . . .

In the atmosphere of Dublin, heavily charged with propaganda,
passion and smouldering memories, such high explosives as Sean
O'Casey handles are bound to detonate. In his latest play, *The Plough
and the Stars*, he brings in the Easter Rebellion of 1916. His critics
reproach him with omitting the heroism and high-minded resolu-
tion, and submerging the ideals of the Rebellion in squalor. In
particular they object to the national flag being carried into a public-
house. The play nearly provoked a riot when it was produced at the
Abbey Theatre, and it was held up one evening while a protest was
made.[1] Yet the leader of the opposition, Mrs Sheehy-Skeffington,
whose husband, Francis Sheehy-Skeffington, was a pacifist martyr
of 1916, has declared in public controversy with Sean O'Casey that

1. The play at a standstill, W. B. Yeats shouted at the rioters from the footlights rebuking them with his scorn: 'Is this,' he asked, 'going to be a recurring
celebration of Irish genius? Synge first, then O'Casey. . . . Dublin has once
more rocked the cradle of genius.' (*Irish Times*, 12 February, 1926, pp. 7–8).

his plays have the 'mark of genius'. O'Casey's own statement is that he views life as a dramatist while his opponents regard it as politicians. He does not claim to write about the heroic side of the struggle, but only of the life he knows. Of the tenement people he has said, 'these people form the bone and sinew and ultimately, I believe, they are going to be the brains, of the country as well.'

In Ireland the issue is one over which writers, politicians and labour men are divided. The controversy should result in closer thought about the place of the poorest workers—the tenement dwellers—within the nation. O'Casey's plays throw a flood of light on obscure realities. But judging by the above statement of his belief, he does not lose sight of bright possibilities, when all this squalor and sordidness are swept away. So *The Plough and the Stars* may be the fittest name for his play.

It is, however, quite wrong to assume that O'Casey has any conscious reforming purpose in his plays. He is putting tenement life before us with its want, poverty, vice, shiftlessness, and all the other evils fostered by bad social conditions. We may draw what moral or conclusion we like. His grim studies of drink and squalor compare favourably with the sickly immorality of the characters in such plays as *Fallen Angels*,[2] for it is not cynicism but human suffering that speaks through O'Casey's work. He is in the tradition of Zola, and of Hauptmann, who brought naturalism to the German stage in *The Weavers* and *The Rats*, which dealt with German working-class life in town and country. He is even more akin to the Russian realists, especially Gorky, who has the same bitter contempt for hazy idealism. Gorky's own plea speaks for O'Casey as well:

Lovers of humanity must not hide the grim truth with the motley words of beautiful lies. Let us face life as it is. All that is good and human in our hearts needs renewing.

It is no wonder that such men, who have had to struggle for physical and intellectual life, become bitter. They are nihilists in the field of thought. *Juno and the Paycock* is comparable in its moving pathos to the shadowy grandeur of W. B. Yeats's *Cathleen ni Houlihan*. But its cry of agony is a cry of disillusion.

After the terrible war-years men have grown to distrust formulas, and O'Casey has seen too many theatrical heroics come crashing to

2. Comedy by Noël Coward, first performed at the Globe Theatre, London, 21 April, 1925.

the ground in a welter of human suffering not to want to dig his knife into bombast and swagger. But this is an age of disillusion, and all we have a right to ask of any dramatist is that he should express an honest view of life. If he does this, then out of anti-idealism will come, when we enter upon another cycle of thought, a finer idealism. O'Casey will have helped to cut away the weeds that always cluster round the flowers of human endeavour.

O'Casey and the Abbey*

EILEEN CROWE †

I had joined the Abbey School of Acting in October, 1921. During the time of the curfew the company was away touring. The Abbey had fallen on bad days and the theatre was closed. Michael Dolan was head of the School of Acting at the time. I think I had thirty shillings a week; the highest salary was four pounds a week—a ridiculously small salary to pay players. But there was no money.

Sean O'Casey's first play, *The Shadow of a Gunman*, was produced in 1923 just after the players—Arthur Shields, Maureen Delany, Gertie Murphy (who married John McCormack's brother) and others —came back from their tour of America and Australia. I heard them talk about the strange man who went to rehearsals, and after the dress rehearsal went around and shook the hand of each of the players, thanking them for appearing in his little play.

I went to the first night of *The Shadow of a Gunman*. At the end of the first act I remember my hands were tingling because I had clapped so much, as had everyone in the audience. I went to the Green Room after the performance and found O'Casey sitting in a corner by himself, looking very frightened. I said to him: 'Are you the author of this play?' He said: 'Yes.' And I said: 'Heavens!' I just couldn't say enough enthusiastic things about it. The next day I had a very lovely letter from him saying that he hadn't realised

* Extracted from Des Hickey and Gus Smith (eds.): *A Paler Shade of Green* (London: Leslie Frewin, 1972), pp. 37–9.

† Abbey actress who starred in several of O'Casey's plays. Married Peter Judge, better known by his stage name of F. J. McCormick, one of the Abbey's most celebrated actors, who also appeared in many of O'Casey's dramas.

when he talked to me the night before that he was talking to the 'Countess Cathleen' and 'Norah Helmer'. We became great friends afterwards, until the break-up. And then a lot of people weren't friends any more.

I played 'Mary Boyle' in the first performance of *Juno and the Paycock* in 1924. Peter Judge played 'Joxer Daly'. It was his great part. When Sydney Morgan played Joxer in London afterwards, he said: 'I can only copy McCormick.' But he liked *The Shadow of a Gunman* best; that was his favourite. After the first night of *Gunman*, Sean O'Casey said to him: 'That wasn't my character. But don't change him. He's much better than the character I wrote.' He and O'Casey were firm friends. O'Casey was quite different from any author the players had met. Peter was the one who befriended him and took him out to meals, partly because he was sorry for him, partly because he liked him and partly because he wanted to talk about the characters in the plays. He considered O'Casey a great playwright, but I remember someone in the Abbey saying to us: 'O'Casey is not a playwright. He's a reporter, and his plays will be forgotten in ten years.'

O'Casey wrote the part of 'The Covey' in *The Plough and the Stars* for Peter, but he was cast as 'Jack Clitheroe'. Peter had been very good to O'Casey in the early days, before he was recognised publicly. But on the fourth night of *The Plough* when the audience were in uproar and Peter, who was one of the cast, was trying to keep them quiet, he said: 'Don't blame the actors. We didn't write this play.' I think O'Casey never forgave him for that.

Forsaking Ireland: The Beginnings of Exile*

Sean O'Casey, the Irish playwright, has parted from Dublin more in sorrow than in anger, and has taken a flat in Kensington [1] on a three years' lease.

* *Irish Independent* (Dublin), 7 July, 1926, p. 9, and *Daily Sketch*, 7 July, 1926, p. 2. Both extracts also appear in *Joseph Holloway's Abbey Theatre*, pp. pp. 269–70.

1. 32 Clareville Street, Chelsea, S.W.7.

'I like London,' he said to a special correspondent last night, 'and London likes me. That's more than I can say of Ireland. I have a good deal of courage, but not much patience, and it takes both courage and patience to live in Ireland. The Irish have no time for those that don't agree with their ideas, and I have no time for those who don't agree with mine. So we decided to compromise, and I am coming here. The English are more tolerant and they believe a lot.

'It may,' he added, 'mean three years' penal servitude for me, but, begorra, it cannot be worse than Dublin.'

*　　　*　　　*

'I am going to write a play about London people,[2] for one thing,' he said. 'Human nature is just the same in a Chelsea environment as in Dublin, but in so many plays about London people one sees only artificial puppets moving. Just as though there was no real tragedy behind the laughter in every life that was ever lived anywhere.

'Besides I have to find a place for my feet somewhere, and people don't seem to like me in Ireland any more. I should not care to write a play about Ireland just now with a possible bitterness in my heart.'

2. *Within the Gates*, published 1933.

Sean O'Casey; or, A Rough Diamond*

BEVERLEY NICHOLS †

He had on a new sky-blue overcoat, and as he took it off, flinging it over the back of his chair, I observed a lining fiercely decorated with red squares. Upon this coat he proceeded to lay his cap, which was of a lighter shade of blue. He then sat down, and buried his face in his hands.

I had lured him to a tea-shop. He had a distinct distaste for more

* From *Are They The Same At Home? Being a Series of Bouquets Differently Distributed* (New York: George H. Doran, 1927), pp. 235-8.
† Author and journalist, who in the twenties gained a reputation as a brilliant and unorthodox interviewer.

exalted places. The tea-shop was filled with a smell of steam and stale rock-cakes. The waitresses raced about, carrying the rock-cakes to pale young men and girls who were seated around us. I have never known a more noisy place. The roar of traffic (which ever and anon increased to deafening point as the door swung open to admit more pale young men), the clattering of tea-cups, the low, moaning conversation of the customers.

Yet it was in such a place that a spell was woven over me by Sean O'Casey, with the weak eyes, the deep-lined cheeks, and the human mouth. It made me forget the noise, the flash of buses outside the dirty windows, everything, except that I was in the presence of a great man. They brought us muffins, and tea, and a plate of cakes; such cakes—cakes like dead sea anemones, with frills round them, cakes with decorations of marzipan and stale cream clinging to them like alien growths. O'Casey looked up and took some tea and a muffin.

'Yesterday,' he said, 'was the happiest day I've spent since I came to England. It was in Hyde Park that I spent it, and I stood there listening to the speakers. I felt almost drunk at the end of it—the characters up there are so rich in comedy.

'*What are your dramatists doing to neglect Hyde Park?*' He smacked his fist on the table, and pointed his muffin at me like a limp bludgeon. I regarded it, fascinated, but did not reply. Then he leant back, his head turned slightly to one side, looked at me out of the corner of his eye, and smiled. 'Why, young man, it's the finest field of character you'll ever know. The people I saw there last night. You listen.'

He bent forward again, and spoke almost in a whisper. 'There was a woman there, a fine woman, standing in the lamplight under the trees. Her voice was very clear and sweet, and she didn't care how many times they interrupted her. All the time she spoke she was patting the crucifix by her side—patting it, fondling it . . . like this . . .

'There was a man there who made a speech about milk. As I stood in the crowd I knew, as soon as he had begun, that he had been making the same speech for years, winter and summer, morning and night. For the people in the front row of the crowd knew it by heart, and began to repeat it with him. He didn't care. He went on —with his chorus. There's a tragedy, and there's a comedy. . . .

'There was a man with a bald head, and little glistening eyes, who spoke of Jesus. There was the light of madness in his eyes, and as I watched him I saw right deep into him, and I knew that he would have killed anybody who refused to be led to Jesus—killed him and thanked his God for the opportunity. . . .

'Then there was a thin man in a black coat, and long grey hair, who kept on taking oranges out of his pocket. He was a vegetarian. There was a man with a mournful voice who spoke of the Lost Tribes. There was every sort of religious mania, dietetic mania, political mania, personal mania. And there it all goes on, night after night, under the trees. But nobody seems to notice it. None of those characters is ever put on to the stage. Why? Tell me why?'

My muffin had now set quite solid, and, on being prodded, felt less obscene than when it first arrived. But I was not really interested in muffins. For opposite me was O'Casey, the ex-slum boy, in 'smart' London. Here he was, with his genius of observation, seeing for the first time the painted ladies, the crimped young men, the poisoned critics, the wilting hectic generation which we have now come to know so well. I was intensely anxious to know how it struck him. And, in order to find out, I asked him about the work of a very brilliant young English dramatist [1] who has specialised in the portrayal of this particular stratum of society.

'Did you ever see *The Vortex*?' [2] I asked O'Casey.

'No. But I read it.'

'Didn't you think it a fine play?'

'No.' Rather fiercely he put five lumps of sugar into his tea-cup. 'The people in it are absolutely artificial.'

'But they're meant to be artificial. If he'd drawn them in any other way, he'd have been telling lies.'

'Nobody's artificial.' O'Casey looked at me kindly, rather as though I were a child who could not quite understand why $a \times a = a^2$.

'Nobody's artificial,' he said. 'Even insects aren't artificial. Shakespeare drew artificial characters, but he gave them humanity. My point about these people is that they haven't got humanity.'

I began to grow almost excited. 'I know they haven't got humanity. They haven't got it on the stage (at least in the first two acts), and they haven't got it in real life. You haven't met them, that's all. I

---

1. Noël Coward (1899–1973).
2. Coward's successful play, first staged in London's West End, at the Royalty Theatre, 16 December, 1924. O'Casey's criticism of Coward, 'Coward Codology', was printed in his book of comments on the contemporary theatre, *The Flying Wasp* (1937). In *Rose and Crown*, later, he refers to Nichols, Coward, etc., as 'a bunch of frolicking fools'.

shouldn't think you particularly wanted to. But if you did meet them, you'd realise what I said was true.'

'If I *did* meet them,' he answered, 'I shouldn't listen to them when they talked like that. I should take them home. I may sit next to a woman at lunch who talks to me politely, and says all the right things. Perhaps she says them very cleverly, but her remarks don't interest me. *She* doesn't begin to live till you see her alone, within four walls. Then she drops all her poses, and she tells you her son is going to marry a woman she hates, or that her lover has left her. She shows all her greeds, her vanities (her *true* vanities), she shows you the things you can love about her, and the things you can hate about her. Isn't that more interesting than mere pose?'

I was not daunted even yet.

'I believe,' I said, 'that these people would pose just as much alone as at a luncheon party. Their whole life is pose. You may say that you would see through their poses. How could you, if the pose was *them*? As one poses, one becomes.'

'I don't believe any human being is devoid of humanity,' said O'Casey. 'If you do, then you're wrong. There's no such thing as inherent artificiality. That's the trouble about half the dramatists today. *They're making life out of drama, instead of making drama out of life.*'

I dropped the point. If there had not been so many crashes going on behind, and if I had not been feeling particularly disillusioned that afternoon, as though I were dwelling in a world of masks, I might have got nearer to an agreement with him. But I still feel he has not yet met these characters which he says are 'artificial', which, to you and me, are so distressingly real.

London Apprentice*

RUPERT CROFT-COOKE †

Once Stanley Hale asked me to do a 'personal interview' with Sean O'Casey whose *Juno and the Paycock* was driving critics and public opinion to delirium. It certainly seemed to me the most exciting thing

* From *The Numbers Came* (London: Putnam, 1963), pp. 159–60.
† Novelist, biographer, essayist; journalist in the twenties.

in the theatre of the time and when Stanley Hale told me he had arranged the interview I was delighted.

The 'personal interview' was rather a thing then and has returned recently, for after a merciful break through the thirties and forties I notice that journalists are again being sent to ask successful playwrights and proletarian novelists all about themselves for the readers of serious Sunday papers, just as Beverley Nichols was sent by the *Sketch* for a series called 'Are They the Same at Home?' Without being invidious I find Beverley's interviews incomparably more searching, effective and entertaining, but concede that he had more interesting material to work on.

I was not in the least entertaining about Sean O'Casey but I was vastly entertained. He lived modestly, in a flat—or was it 'rooms'? [1] —in Chelsea. The pretence of an interview was soon forgotten if, in fact, he had ever taken it seriously. He was a kindly, generous, natural person who refused to accept any role but his own, that of a Dublin labourer and patriot who had suddenly achieved phenomenal success. He did not play this up or allow it to be used for publicity purposes but made no attempt to conceal it.

'He speaks,' I wrote in my priggish little interview afterwards,[2] 'of the time when he felt the "old nationalist animus" and would only spell his name O'Cathasaigh as though such hot-headed days were done.' I seem to have got nothing else publishable from him except his admiration for Goya (which I should have expected) and a bit about his life in Dublin which he has since written far better himself. But I remember very clearly how he gave me a meal in an Italian restaurant nearby and showed a play I had written to Sir Barry Jackson,[3] though he thought it 'no bloody good' himself. And I remember a story he told me, not to illustrate his contempt for publicity-seeking but just as a story.

On St Patrick's day, it appeared, he arrived at the theatre to find J. B. Fagan and a number of press photographers waiting for him. On the table was a pile of shamrock—'You know, they think over here I *eat* the stuff.' Fagan bustled up and said he thought it would be a happy idea if they could have a picture of Sean O'Casey pinning a bunch of shamrock on Sara Allgood's breast. (She was playing

1. A flat, as Eileen O'Casey relates in *Sean*.
2. *Theatre World* (London), 5, no. 21 (October, 1926), p. 10.
3. Director, manager and dramatist; founder of the Malvern Festival, where many of Shaw's plays were staged.

'Juno'.) 'You can have it if you want it,' said O'Casey, 'but it's pinning it on her arse I'll be and not on her breast at all.' That could not go into my 'interview' which would have been immeasurably the better for it, nor could his remark about Wilde, 'I never thought he had a fair deal from this gang o' whores over here.'

We travelled on the top of a bus through Sloane Square and looking at the memorial there he said, 'That has given me a title for a play—*The Sword on the Cross*.[4]

I thought him a big man by any measurement and though I failed to convey it in what I wrote afterwards, I have never changed that opinion.

4. Another leg-pull: O'Casey never wrote a play with this title.

'Shakespeare was my Education': Interview with the Author of *The Silver Tassie**

GEORGE WALTER BISHOP †

The story of Mr Sean O'Casey is a modern epic: the Dublin labourer who, after spending night after night at the Abbey Theatre, eventually wrote plays which are among the greatest of the century. I had seen him on the stage when, after one of his first nights, the immaculately dressed, urbane manager introduced a shy young man in a tweed suit and a cardigan, who blinked at the audience and then fled into the wings. Then I saw him again in his own home at St John's Wood,[1] where for two hours he talked to me about his own and other people's plays—mostly the latter.

The first impression on entering the room was of the magnificent

* *The Observer* (London), 6 October, 1929, p. 13, originally entitled '*The Silver Tassie*: Interview with Mr Sean O'Casey', by 'G.W.B.'.
† English dramatic critic and author (1886–1965). Theatre Correspondent of *The Observer* (1928–32) and also of the *Daily Telegraph* (1932–7). Literary Editor, *Daily Telegraph*, from 1937 until his death. Editor of the stage newspaper, *The Era* (1928–31).

1. 19 Woronzow Road, London, N.W.8.

Augustus John portrait over the mantelpiece, and the second was that everything else approximated in taste to the picture. The books on the shelves were Shakespeare and the other Elizabethan playwrights, volumes of the Restoration dramatists, Balzac, Nietzsche. Then O'Casey came in. He was dressed in a grey sweater, and I realised how remarkably John had caught the man in the portrait.

We began, of course, with *The Silver Tassie*, which Mr C. B. Cochran is presenting at the Apollo on Friday, 11 October, 1929.[2] He was full of enthusiasm for Mr Cochran,[3] 'that rare combination of artist and man of the theatre', for Mr Raymond Massey, who is producing *The Tassie* (as he calls it) and 'enters more fully into the play than I do myself', and for Mr Charles Laughton and the rest of the company. 'It is a difficult play,' he said, 'because in one of the scenes I have attempted something which has never been done on the stage before. One of Mr Yeats's objections [4] to the play was that it contained no dominating character, and for that reason I feel it is a better play than *Juno and the Paycock* (which is the poorest thing I have had produced) and *The Plough and the Stars*. In *The Tassie* the tragedy dominates the characters.'[5]

*   *   *

'Although the full correspondence with the Abbey Theatre had been published [6] certain newspapers have stated that *The Silver Tassie* was not produced in Dublin because I refused to accept Mr Yeats's suggestions and make some alterations in the play. In other words they make me out an impossible creature. I should be glad if you will correct this. In his letter to me written on 20 April, 1928, Mr Yeats said: "I cannot advise you to amend the play. . . . I see nothing for it but a new theme." I am anxious to make it clear that I am not a high-and-mighty dramatist who thinks that his plays cannot be improved. On the first night it will be seen that certain of Mr Massey's

2. The play was published in 1928, soon after its rejection by the Abbey Theatre Directorate.

3. So, also, was Shaw: Letter to *The Times*, 26 November, 1929.

4. Yeats had written: 'The play is all anti-war propaganda' (Letter to O'Casey, 20 April, 1928), though, as Hugh MacDiarmid, in *The Company I've Kept* (London, 1966), p. 163, says: 'Yeats did not keep Irish Nationalist propaganda out of his poems.'

5. Lady Gregory, *Journals*, pp. 107-8, complained that the characters in *The Silver Tassie* had become 'lay figures, lantern slides, showing the horror of war.' Only by so impersonalising could the author achieve his ideal purpose.

6. *Observer* (London), 3 June, 1928, p. 19.

suggestions have been accepted; the production will differ slightly from the version published by Macmillan.

'I was interested in St John Ervine's article in *The Observer* on the use of the aside in modern drama. Playwrights and managers are afraid of so many things and think too much of their audiences. They are afraid of soliloquy and pause in drama, and I believe that audiences are not as stupid as dramatists imagine. I am irritated by being told of the things I must not do in plays.'

I asked him if he had written any new plays.

*   *   *

'I am incapable of starting a new play until the last one is produced. After *The Tassie* is staged I shall lose interest in it, except that it provides me with money (and I want money as much as anybody), and start on something else. I have two or three ideas, and one came when I watched the supers during the rehearsals for *The Tassie*. I am writing some short stories [7] based on characters I have met. Some time ago I started to turn *Juno* into a novel, but I dropped it. I couldn't do it. I have also written part of an autobiography, which will be finished and published some time.' [8]

We talked of modern dramatists. 'England is waiting for the great English dramatist who will write about his own people. The playwrights of today turn out tiny plays about little society ladies and gentlemen with scraps of photographic dialogue. They throw life out of focus. Hardly any of them attempt to portray the life of today with imagination and passion. Recently I read in an article which offered advice to young playwrights that Mr Noël Coward and Mr Frederick Lonsdale should be studied. Shakespeare, the Elizabethans, the Restoration dramatists, and Shaw are the men to study.

*   *   *

'I would make it a penal offence,' Mr O'Casey continued, 'for any man to write a play without being able to declaim two or three of Shakespeare's plays by heart. Shakespeare was my education. When I was a boy in Dublin thirty years ago, the Benson Company came to the city, and I spent all my small wages and went without food in order to see all the plays that were performed. I could hardly read or write at the time.'

'That was your first interest in the drama?' I asked.

7. Published, later, in *Windfalls* (1934).   8. *I Knock at the Door* (1939).

'Yes, I suppose it was in me, somehow. I learned to read by Shakespeare and used to act the plays in my room'—here O'Casey gave me a scene from *Julius Caesar*—'and when I was seventeen, I wrote a comedy called *Withered Heather*. Some time after that I belonged to the Drama group in the National Club. The members were content to imitate the Abbey Players, perform the same plays, in order to become little Arthur Sinclairs.[9] I suggested that it would be a good idea to play something that had never been acted before, and I wrote *Frost in the Flower*, a two-act comedy based on a family in the club. It was so near to the characters that it was never performed, but the play was sent to the Abbey and the directors sent me a detailed criticism. That was really my start. Afterwards I wrote *The Harvest Festival* and *The Crimson in the Tri-colour*, and then *The Shadow of a Gunman*, which was eventually produced at the Abbey.'

9. A reference to the Irish actor, husband of Maire O'Neill, who was with the Abbey Theatre until 1916, playing in all the notable productions of that time.

Remembrance of Things Past: On Meeting Sean O'Casey*

LESLIE REES

At the University of Western Australia I had done considerable reading on the modern Irish drama movement. Sean O'Casey was at that time the most recent upthrusting genius of the Irish theatre: the turbulent row with Yeats, following O'Casey's departure from Dublin for the shores of perfidious but welcoming Albion, had occurred only a few years before my own arrival in London in 1930. *The Silver Tassie* had been taken up by C. B. Cochran, having been refused for the Abbey Theatre by Yeats—one of the most serious errors of judgement a theatre director has ever made, for it denied O'Casey to Ireland. Cochran presented the play in glory at a West

* *Meanjin Quarterly* (Melbourne), 24, no. 4 (December 1964), pp. 414–20. One of O'Casey's poems, 'Saintly Sinner, Sing for Us', appeared in *Meanjin Quarterly*, 10, no. 2 (Winter 1951), p. 144, and previously in the *New Statesman* (London), 16 December, 1950.

End theatre. It lost money but won esteem. And O'Casey, the child of the Dublin streets, the underfed bricklayer's labourer of the tenements, once employed at twenty-five bob a week, the amateur writer who had remade the fortunes of the Abbey Theatre with *The Shadow of a Gunman, Juno and the Paycock* and *The Plough and the Stars*, now had an address in genteel St John's Wood—at 19 Woronzow Road.

I knew this because from Perth I'd been briefly in touch with him. I had written requesting answers to a few questions about his work and background. Sent in his own scrawling hand, his reply about schooling was classical:

> I have never received any education in the technical nonsense of the word but, teaching myself first to choose teachers, have been gently and generously taught by Shakespeare, Milton, Keats, Shelley, Balzac, Whitman, Strindberg and a crowd of others.

Of all writers then in Britain, Shaw and O'Casey most surely stimulated my idolatrous feelings. Shaw was a universal prophet and 'dramatic emperor of Europe' (as he modestly described himself) while O'Casey was the voice of Ireland and, through Ireland, of mankind. Having read nearly all the Irish plays produced since the nineties when the Irish Literary Theatre began to burgeon, I was willing to swear by O'Casey as the finest interpreter of life and character of them all. He was an elemental spirit, a savage and unrelenting flayer of hypocrisy, cant and war-murder, indeed of all that is mean and traitorous in human institutions and the human breast. At the same time I felt that his compassion, more particularly for women, was real and abiding. And then there was that Falstaffian comic gusto. Where in drama could one find such alternations of the poignant and the irresistibly absurd, both in situations and speech! The Celt in me was gratefully ignited by the fiery flame that was O'Casey. In his slum plays (which were all that he had written up to that time) I was well aware of faults of half-baked form, but the fervour and vehemence of the man, expressed in hammering angry phrases or droll cascading images, surely outbalanced formal ineptitude, in fact rendered it unimportant and trivial. His best plays seemed to me to have qualities of passion and 'rhythmic realism' absent from nearly every dramatic work since the Elizabethans.

In London, after months of delay, some impulse caused me not to write but to take a bus to St John's Wood and knock at his front door.

It was a solid ugly door on an unattractive semi-detached house built close to the street. A middle-aged woman opened the door. From her voice and manner I judged her an Irish servant but I couldn't be sure. I asked to see Mr O'Casey. After some delay—during which I was able to note that the walls of the passage-hall were hung with large reproductions of paintings by Degas, Gauguin and Van Gogh—an attractive young woman came and said that she was Mrs O'Casey. I introduced myself and said that, having had a letter from O'Casey, I hoped to be able to meet him. Keeping me on the front mat she went away, then returned and said in a rather business-like way, the way of an important person's wife: 'Mr O'Casey is writing now: would you like to come here for tea on Sunday? I'll try to get him away from his work for an hour.' Dancing with unbelief I groped my way toward the bus stop.

On the Sunday at 4 p.m. I was on the doorstep again and the servant-dear immediately led me into a small lounge room, furnished with comfortable, modern-minded settee and armchairs. It was a pleasant and tasteful room, with an outlook on a small green back-garden. A fire was burning. Over the mantle was a large portrait of O'Casey. I thought I recognised it as the Augustus John painting reproduced in a volume of O'Casey's plays: actually it was a full-size sketch for that painting.[1]

After a few minutes in came Sean O'Casey, the picture of informality, in an old pair of grey flannel trousers, a brown guernsey with tie hanging awry, thick socks and slippers. As I rose he came up to me, walking rather uncertainly and peering forward. Perhaps he couldn't see clearly: I knew his sight was bad and he was wearing large glasses with silver rims. His beady brown eyes seemed incredibly small behind the spectacles.

In a quiet unassertive mumbling tone O'Casey motioned me to a seat. He seemed to be trying to get the hang of me. 'So you've come all the way from Australia?' The voice was raw Dublin, thin and whining, not attractive like the best Irish tones. 'Tell me about Australia.' He relaxed on a sofa and put his feet up. I could hardly believe my ears. Here in England a resident was asking me to talk about Australia. This had scarcely happened before: the even unruffled capacity of the English educated classes for *not* being curious about a stranger and his background was one of the things that most

1. A coloured reproduction appears on the cover of the paperback edition of *Sean*, by Eileen O'Casey (London: Pan Books, 1973).

defeated me. It appeared at once that O'Casey, although living on English soil, was far from being absorbed into English ways. I looked with growing appreciation at his rough and ugly face, his thin denuded cheeks, his long protruding nose and the untidy hair that was mousy in front and skimpy-bald on the back of the skull.

About Australia he seemed to know nothing except the geographical position. This ignorance was no novelty in Britain so a few facts lubricated the opening movements of our conversation. Before long his wife came in, chic and dainty, with her West End voice that was not quite West End. And the wordless old duck of a servant brought in afternoon tea.

Mrs O'Casey was addressed by her husband as Eileen. She scarcely seemed true to the expected picture. O'Casey must have been about 46 years of age, she about 26. Was she part of the fruits of his success? Such a person did not seem to have emerged from a tenement background. From conversation she would be Irish-born but the manner was English. They spoke of a boy,[2] aged about 18 months. In fact the boy was now to be seen in the back garden, looked after by a nurse. The patterns were neither slum Dublin nor standard St John's Wood. But despite discrepancies all was domestic harmony and light. O'Casey showed a lively interest in his son. So did I, always a good move in people's homes I'd found. Eileen revealed that she was an actress and singer. At present she had a chorus part in the long-running Noël Coward musical, *Bitter-Sweet*.

My 'hour' was slipping away in small-talk not connected with O'Casey's plays. I wanted to steer him on to this vital subject but he was reluctant, bored with it. He talked warmly and abundantly and with a broad simpleness about other people's plays and books, using his low mumbly voice not very eloquently but always with decision. Shakespeare came into the talk often: O'Casey was all for quoting long passages from *Hamlet* and *Julius Caesar* but usually dried up after a few pentameters and turned to me with the words 'What is it? What is it?', an appeal that to my chagrin I never seemed able to gratify. Sometimes in quoting he would interpolate 'There's a loovely loine', the brogue now coming over more richly as he smiled and peered in my direction.

When at last I asked 'Do you think *Juno* the best of your plays?' he said in an offhand way: 'No. I hate *Juno*. Tired of it. *The Silver Tassie* every time.' He went on denigrating *Juno and the Paycock*.

2. Breon O'Casey, b. 1928.

He was tired of making characters like 'Captain' Boyle and Mrs Madigan . . . too easy. It was the purpose in his work he found hard to express.

I reflected that in one act of *The Silver Tassie* O'Casey had become the consciously literary playwright, no longer using the Dublin vernacular heightened by his native gift of humour and rhythm: rather going after inner revelation by poetic statement. Any author would have been stimulated by such adventures in stylistic writing: O'Casey was much involved with them now, not that he seemed able or had the desire to discuss them in detail.

I mentioned the question of facility. His plays, I said, seemed to flow along in tidal waves of energy. 'Wrong,' he said. Writing was a great labour. It took him twelve months of spare time to write *Juno*. He further illustrated his pondering thought and trial-by-error craftsmanship by telling how, when some alterations were required during rehearsals of *The Tassie*, he had to bring the script home before he could adjust it. 'Somerset Maugham would have slipped the new words in on the spot,' he said.

'Do you take your characters from life?' O'Casey would not be drawn but Eileen let a cat halfway out of a Dublin building labourer's lunchbag when she interpolated: 'You did know someone like "Captain" Boyle, Sean?' Even then, O'Casey declined to amplify.

We discussed plays recently on in London. He denounced *Journey's End*. 'A bad play!' I had been brought under its spell and felt bound to defend it. 'It's a bad play,' O'Casey repeated, his voice rising in anger. The taste of lemon came into my mouth. 'It's a good play,' I said with equal vehemence. 'It's a *bad* play,' said O'Casey crushingly.

He did not give reasons. Afterwards I reflected that his dislike of *Journey's End* could have come from the class-conscious element in Sherriff's outlook, implying, or running the risk of implying, that the only soldiers worth taking seriously were the officers, not the rank and file.[3] O'Casey's own bitter war scene in *The Tassie* was of course markedly different, although criticised by Yeats as not based on personal experience and therefore not good. Any comparative thoughts on the subject of *The Tassie* were unstated but the sparks had flown between us for a few seconds and I wondered whether

3. O'Casey returns to the subject in *Rose and Crown*: '. . . the stench of blood hid in a mist of soft-sprayed perfume'.

O'Casey was now going to throw me out as a cheeky young intruder. But conversation resumed and no harm done.

There was another slight passage of hackling warmth when the baby was once more mentioned. Mrs O'Casey on slight encouragement told me of the child's bright ways and O'Casey during this period sat in silence. Suddenly he said with trenchant vigour: 'And we won't be sending him to one of those damned universities.' I demurred, being fresh from university myself, though I'd been but a humble part-time student earning my way. 'No university education,' said O'Casey dangerously. 'Hotbeds of snobbery for the privileged classes.' I asked leave to tell something about the University of Western Australia where at that time no fees were charged any scholar and anybody from the entire state population was welcome provided he could pass his examinations. O'Casey was impressed: he cooled down and finished by mumbling: 'Well, it might be a good thing for him to go to that sort of university after all . . . it might be good for him to mix with different people like that.' I felt I'd won a worthwhile round.

At about six o'clock Mrs O'Casey seemed to grow restive so I said 'I'd better be going now.' But O'Casey at once put in, 'Come up to my room for half an hour.' I said, 'So long as I'm not in the way,' and O'Casey replied, with humorous directness, 'We'll tell you when you're in the way.' His wife thereupon asked me if I'd like to stay to dinner. I was certainly anxious to probe into more of the O'Casey story though without thought of journalistic exploitation. The O'Caseys were not treating me as an interviewer.

O'Casey and I now went upstairs to a little room, furnished with shelves of books (there were two full bookcases downstairs), a small desk, an armchair and a narrow bed against one wall. He said, from between lips that hardly moved, 'This is where I work.' I sat in the armchair and had a cigarette and O'Casey lolled at full length on the bed: at that moment he hardly looked the hard-toiling type.

I eventually persuaded him to talk about the subject of his plays and he told me the story of his beginnings. There was that first book he wrote, a little history of a trades union movement.[4] 'I got £15 for that and the cheque came as my mother lay dead. I couldn't get it changed, people thought it suspicious I should have had a cheque for so much money, in fact a cheque at all. It was crossed and had to be

4. *The Story of the Irish Citizen Army* (1919); reprinted in *Feathers from the Green Crow*, pp. 180–239.

paid into a bank and I hadn't a bank account. A friend got it changed and most of it went on the funeral. When the undertaker came to the house he said, "No bloody money, no bloody funeral." [5] Just like that. But I had the money.'

As O'Casey drawled out this tale, extracting with a half-smile the full flavour of cynicism and irony, I wondered how far that dead mother of his (obviously a very important influence in his life) might have been identified with Juno, the universal, deep-suffering mother in his greatest work. And yet she must have been a mother capable of lighter moods. Hadn't he dedicated the book version of one [6] of his plays to '*The gay laugh of my mother at the gate of the grave.*'?

Still lying on the daybed in the near-darkness, he was in the full swing of reminiscence now. He told me about the little Dublin Labour Group which ran an acting society. It was always producing the plays (not very good at that time) lately seen at the Abbey. 'I said to the members, "Why don't you get away from the Abbey stuff?" and when they raised their eyebrows I said, "I'll write you a play!" Well, I wrote a play round the lives of an actual family in the Labour Group and the committee turned it down, afraid. So I sent it to the Abbey and they turned it down too. I wrote one or two more plays and sent them to the Abbey. They kept one for two years promising to produce it and I told various people I was going to have a play done there. And then they turned it down. Well, I sent them one more. This was *The Shadow of a Gunman.* They said they would produce it, I think as a sort of compensation for turning down the other one. Just as well! If it had been turned down too, I don't think I'd have tackled any more plays.'

'It was put on for the last three nights of the season. The first night there was a house of £20, the second night £35. The last night was house full. So the Abbey began its next season with *The Gunman.* And it filled the theatre again.

'I wrote a new short play [7] and it was produced at the Abbey. It was a good one and yet was received in stony silence. I couldn't understand this. That night I went home and began *Juno and the Paycock.*'

The Irish servant came up the stairs to say dinner was ready and we went to the small dining-room in the basement. Here the three of us sat to a meal of roast lamb and vegetables and a bottle of white

5. Lady Gregory, *Journals*, pp. 77–8.   6. *The Plough and the Stars.*
7. *Cathleen Listens In.*

wine. As soon as our plates were before us O'Casey bent over and began eating without ceremony. 'Go on,' he signalled me. No passing of the wine clockwise here. I liked the homeliness of it all. It was a quiet meal, with Mrs O'Casey and myself now doing most of the talking—some of it about Australian life. I told them about the Perth Repertory Club production of *The Paycock* in which there'd been fine renderings of Boyle and Juno by Tom Tracy and Molly Ick, respectively. 'Oh yes, I heard about that show,' said O'Casey to my surprise.

After dinner we sat in the lounge room before the fire. I didn't leave until 10.45. O'Casey helped me into my coat. I'd already told him that my fiancée Coralie had written a short play which was produced in Perth (with herself in the leading rôle) and published in *The Black Swan*—the first play, so far as I know, ever to be published in Western Australia. O'Casey cheered me by saying, 'You might like to bring her out.' I said goodnight to his wife and O'Casey walked with me to the bus corner, giving repeated directions as to how to get home. As the bus came in sight he said, 'Ring me in a fortnight and come out again. I might have another friend.'

Despite rancorous moments he'd been a much milder man than I had expected, with touches of gentleness and courtesy, a rough diamond only by bourgeois English standards. There had been few outbursts of spirits or energy to reflect the boisterous humour of his plays. During the whole evening I don't think he once laughed aloud, though ironic comedy expressed itself in wry verbal comment. He seemed far from physically strong, was even frail, flat-chested. But his positive nature revealed itself through his sense of enquiry, his spontaneous curiosity. As to the reticent anglo-saxon middle-class life that was all around us, obviously he was a fish out of its true element. For want of a better, he had immersed himself in another element which he was prepared to accept but not necessarily to approve. At mention of cricket test matches he at once made it clear that he backed the Australians: this merely out of an Irishman's automatic rejection of England. I am sure that our common lack of liking for the alien English caste system was a bond between him and me. Egalitarian Australianism matched egalitarian Irishism. On the way home I couldn't have been more exhilarated.

O'Casey in Buckinghamshire*

J. L. HODSON †

Ireland, I have often thought, was created by the Almighty to entertain the world, and Irishmen to lighten our darkness. George Leach
of the *Manchester Guardian* used to say somebody ought to put a
row of footlights round the country. It is difficult for Irishmen to
open their mouths without uttering something worth while. Not
only is this true of men like Bernard Shaw and Sean O'Casey, our
two best living British dramatists, but of J. M. N. Jeffries and James
Dunn, two of the wittiest men who ever trod Fleet Street. I believe
it was Dunn who invented the joke, apropos of the army poster 'Join
the R.A.F. and see the world'—'Join the R.I.C. (Royal Irish Constabulary) and see the next world.' When Jeffries and I were together
in Belfast he said to me, 'There are only two sorts of people here—
those who make handkerchiefs and those who don't use them'; and
walking down the streets of Criccieth he remarked, 'The inventors
of standardisation were the Welsh. They started by standardising
their names.'

Six years ago I was sent to Dublin because ructions were expected
on Armistice Day. Half the places I went to in those days had just
distinguished themselves by having a row or were about to do so. An
old reporter said to me the other day with almost a break in his voice,
'I could have cried when I went to Eastbourne on that murder. It
was the only lovely town in England that wasn't associated in my
mind with a crime. Now there isn't a single beauty spot left for me.'
Well, Dublin duly threw its stink bombs and hurled a few stones
and broke a few college windows and tore down a few Union Jacks.
Nothing very much, as Ireland goes; and next day, having a few
hours to spare, I sought Sean O'Casey. He had never been to England then nor had his *Juno and the Paycock* been performed in Lon-

---

* From *No Phantoms Here* (London: Faber, 1932), pp. 147-56. The chapter
is entitled, 'Sean O'Casey', and is an expanded version of the interview, 'The
Strange Mystery of Sean O'Casey', published in *News Chronicle* (London), 21
December, 1931, p. 6.

It seems clear from this interview that Hodson is the author of the previous
anonymous interview, 'The Author of *Juno*: An Informal Talk' (1925).

† English journalist, dramatist and novelist (1891-1956).

don. I paid two visits to the Abbey Theatre before I got his address [1]
—O'Casey didn't like to be called on in his tenement lodging, they
said—he would probably be annoyed. I walked up and down the
North Circular Road which seemed about five miles long this grey
afternoon with mist curling in the shadows. Shopkeepers and drovers
had never heard of him. They knew of O'Caseys who drove tramcars,
or slaughtered cattle, or sold newspapers, or laboured at the docks,
but O'Caseys who wrote plays, 'Sure, they'd never heard of such a
t'ing. Wouldn't it be Shamus O'Casey who played the cornet I'd be
wantin'?'

About five o'clock I found the house—a tall, gloomy house, dirty
grey, with peeling plaster, and stone passage—the sort you find in
any slum. I knocked at the first door down the hall on the left. A
man in shirt-sleeves opened it about six inches. Was he Sean
O'Casey? He was. Could I speak to him? He didn't think so—he was
getting dressed. I told him who I was. He was not impressed by me
or by my newspaper, the *Daily Mail*. He had no time to talk about
plays—he was going down town to see a girl. But I hadn't tramped
up and down the five-miles-long North Circular Road for nothing. I
kept on talking and O'Casey's natural courtesy gave in.

It was a curious meeting. He continued in the half dark groping
about, getting dressed, and I sat down and fired questions at him. I
told him his Dublin critics said he went about with a notebook and
pencil jotting down things he heard, and that he only wrote about
what he knew of. He would pause, and stop groping and ask firmly,
'What in the name o' God *should* I write about? What did Euripides
and Aristophanes write about? Born in a tenement house, I write
about 'em. If *Juno* is a success in London, I'll leave this place for
good.' He tore the world's hypocrisies—besides handfuls of contemporaries—to pieces with searing, cynical tongue and bitter
humour. He thought little in those days of folk like Noël Coward
and John Galsworthy. 'You can't turn life into a comedy in one play
and into a tragedy in another,' he said. 'Life isn't like that. We have
our happy moments and our sad moments'; and again he said, 'If
you want to find the play that is in people, you must follow them
home.' He used the words of a writer and the accent of a workman,
a soft, broad, Irish brogue.

In this room he slept, ate, worked and lived his life, cooking his
meals himself—a piece of bacon, a few potatoes. He had an old tall

1. 422 North Circular Road, Dublin.

typewriter, bought second-hand, and home-made bookshelves crammed with books—Shakespeare, the first book he ever bought, Milton—stuff like that. His desk he carried home in three pieces to save cartage.

I said, 'They say you break all the rules in writing a play.'

'So did Shakespeare,' he said, thrusting out his sharp chin and peering at me from short-sighted, weak eyes. He worked in those days in penny school exercise books, and then typed and re-typed until he got it right. He had to hold a manuscript three inches from his nose to read it. Sometimes he wrote a one-act play as diversion, but a three-act play—that took a long time and a great many ideas, he said.

He pulled on his heavy boots, a trench coat, and a cap down over his eyes and we walked down into the centre of Dublin together. He might have been a bricksetter's labourer, or a gunman. But he talked with remarkable wit, and insight, and was extraordinarily incisive in his opinions. He seemed to suffer from no doubts. Education? Education was a great drawback to a dramatist. He told me about his early life—how he was half starved till nine years old, living on dry bread and tea, how he learnt his lessons in the streets of Dublin, taught himself to read at fourteen, and then earned four shillings a week in an ironmonger's; how next year he was working fifteen hours a day for nine shillings a week at a newsvendor's. Afterwards he navvied, carried bricks and did odd jobs for fifteen years. For ten of those years he visited the Abbey Theatre—pit or gallery—read Shakespeare, and wrote plays that were rejected. Part of the time he was on the dole. His first success was *The Shadow of a Gunman*, written largely out of his own experience. But it wasn't until *Juno* caught on that he gave up his manual work. 'I decided then,' he said, 'that one job is enough for any man.'

I asked him if he had any idea how much he was likely to earn if *Juno* proved a success in London. No, he had no idea. Some of the play characters were real—he had worked with 'Captain' Johnny Boyle—hadn't even altered his name. No, Boyle was not a theatregoer, and hadn't seen the play. O'Casey was doing a small amount of prose-writing for the Irish weeklies, but when I mentioned novel-writing he was scornful. No, he would never write a novel; any damn fool could write a novel. (A few months later I told Arnold Bennett, sitting in the stalls of a theatre, what O'Casey said. He looked solemnly to his front and said, with his stammer, '*I* don't find it so —so—damned easy.') By this time we had tramped to the middle of Dublin and O'Casey left me abruptly to keep his appointment in a teashop, this bachelor of forty-four whose genius was flowering.

Next time I saw him was in 1931. He met me as I got off a bus at the corner of a lane in Chalfont St Giles, Buckinghamshire. I had written asking if I might visit him, for I was eager to know what he was doing, and I found him awaiting me. As I rode down I had pondered about him. Since we had met he had been awarded the Hawthornden Prize for *Juno*, had failed to write *The Red Lily*, a play about a prostitute that he had told me in Dublin was to be his next work, and had had his *Silver Tassie* rejected by the Abbey Theatre and produced by C. B. Cochran. And after that—silence. No play from O'Casey. Had his genius deserted him, his inspiration dried up now Dublin was left behind? Or was it going into his tongue instead of his pen?

I saw a man standing there and for a moment hesitated. He wore a wideawake hat, a brown guernsey to the throat like a fisherman, a Harris tweed suit, and strong boots. He looked at me from behind gold-rimmed spectacles, we spoke and turned down the road. 'Watch the way,' he said. 'I can't see well enough to come back with you after dark.'

A swan sailed the wayside pond, smoke curled in the windless air above the brown brick cottages, and there was the smell of burning wood and rubbish. He told me with deep content that England is lovely beyond his belief, that he likes the quiet, sober people. No, he would never go back to Dublin except on a visit. We passed John Milton's cottage; William Penn's house, he said, was over the hill. On a small rising stood his brick bungalow, with two acres of ground and an orchard. O'Casey likes to dig there and work in the garden, and when he isn't digging or walking about the countryside to work at his old desk on the old typewriter. A portrait of him by Augustus John with something of O'Casey's wild, bold character in its flamboyant colour, hangs on the wall. I thought his tongue was keen but less saw-edged, his humour as deep but with greater breadth than when we had met in Dublin. He looked well and talked, with something of the air of a master, of plays, books, films and wireless. Would wireless develop into an art form? He doubted it. Had I heard the broadcast performance of *Julius Caesar* the other night? He thought it was terrible. He had sung a Litany calling down the wrath o' God on them.

I asked him where the *Red Lily* was, and what he was working at. He laughed that I had been taken in. There never had been a *Red Lily*, he said, nor was there ever such a play in his intention. He had told people that to put them off—they were always pestering him in those days. One may add they still do. Every time anything is said about his working on a play people write asking if they may see it. I found he has kept an Irish and boyish love of being contrary and says a good many things for devilment; and that he is disputatious and fond of argument.

He didn't want to talk about his work, but he owned he is writing a new play about London life;[2] which part of London he wouldn't say. First, he said, he thought he would write it straight for the films,[3] but again he changed his mind. He is half-way through a sort of biography[4] too, and has done a number of sketches—'weaving a pattern' he called it. He works very slowly, writing and re-writing —never pens even a letter without great care.

Six years ago he had told me he could write plays better because he was never educated; now he described that as nonsense. 'Even now,' he said, 'I don't know the English language.' I asked him which part of the day he does his writing in, but it was his wife who answered. 'He starts about midnight,' she said, 'and goes on tap-tapping at the machine till two or three in the morning.'

We had tea, and his son, Breon, aged three, extremely Irish-looking, came in and looked round with the wise comprehension of that age and departed without speaking.

Mrs O'Casey said, 'Sean has read your play. Ask him what he thinks about it.' But he demurred. 'I don't like reading work by men I'm going to meet, especially plays. I wouldn't like to express any opinion that might influence them.' We talked a good deal after tea. He seems to have no doubts about anything and I suspect that when he has, he becomes even more downright to entertain you or stir you up.

Here are some of his assertions:

That we need a chain of municipal theatres;

That he is sick of people talking about *Juno and the Paycock*— 'it was a good enough play for a man just beginning, but no more than that';

That our finest English dramatist today is Granville Barker;

2. *Within the Gates* ('A Fantasy of the Seasons in Hyde Park').
3. Hitchcock was interested in the idea at first—*Rose and Crown* (1952), p. 154.
4. *I Knock at the Door*.

That he can find Joxer Dalys (one of his *Juno* characters)—wheedling, drunken, deceitful, cowardly—anywhere;

That he's finished with Dublin as a play subject—'To be creative, you must pass on to something fresh';

The he can't be bothered to insert emendations to *The Silver Tassie* —which he admits has its faults;

That you can't write except from within your experience, and that Shakespeare and Milton were no exceptions to that;

That a newspaper has more abiding influence on people than a war;

That no young dramatist should take advice from an older one;

That the old novel form is dead and that the few writers really 'alive' include James Joyce and Aldous Huxley;

That the theatre also needs a new art form;

That a hard upbringing is no help to a writer, but the contrary. (This arose from my saying that it was curious that two other playwrights I know well, James R. Gregson, the Yorkshire dramatist, and Ernest George, author of *Down our Street*, had very tough beginnings too, both earning a living when still children, and that I doubted if they would ever have written so well had their childhood been smooth and the road flat to their feet.)

He was almost gay when, taking his wife's arm to guide him, the two of them walked back to the bus with me. I said, 'I could have sworn that in Dublin your eyes were brown. And now they are blue. Was I mistaken?'

No, it was very likely so, he said. They change colour with the treatment for his short-sightedness. Blue is their true colour. 'You know,' his wife said, 'Sean was practically blind for years and had his eyes bandaged. He puts that down to being half-starved as a boy.' His greatest joys happen to be reading Shakespeare and looking at good pictures, so it's a peculiarly harsh stroke that Fate has dealt him. Yet he not only made no mention of that but struck me as being profoundly content; and he made me proud of our English countryside and its people who have influenced him so. He sees men working on the road—one of his old jobs—and a rush of the old wish to be with them comes over him. 'Every man should work with his hands three months in every twelve,' he said, as we trudged through the darkness.

We stood waiting for the bus. The night wind was chill and he had no overcoat. I asked them not to wait—he would catch cold. But he had strong views on that, too—'No man,' he said, 'can catch cold

by going without his shirt. I've tried it and proved it'—and he
wouldn't be shaken on the point.

The bus swung round the corner, lights blazing. 'Oh,' I said, 'I've
forgotten to ask you what your ambitions are.'

'Ambitions?' he grinned. 'That the next may be a great play—
and *not* to send the boy to Oxford.'

American Interlude: O'Casey in New York[*]

BOSLEY CROWTHER [†]

It had been carefully explained beforehand that Sean O'Casey, the
Irish dramatist and author of the play, *Within the Gates*, which will
have its American première in New York, at the National Theatre,[1]
preferred not to be disturbed—especially by strangers—during rehearsals. It was a justifiable preference. He desired to be alone and
unmolested, free to concentrate his senses upon the stage. Only by
special dispensation was an inquisitive visitor granted permission to
intrude upon his solitude.

But when the visitor arrived at the theatre Mr O'Casey was nowhere to be found. He had apparently impelled himself by some
Celtic charm to vanish. No one seemed to know where he had gone.
On the stage a young woman director was marshalling a sober procession of ten or twelve actors and actresses across an inclined platform behind the figure of a massive war memorial. They were the
Down-and-Outers within the gates and they chanted a sonorous
dirge as they plodded disconsolately along. Mr O'Casey was not
among them. Nor had he yet appeared when the young director
called a sudden halt of the procession, bitingly reproved her charges

* *New York Times*, 14 October, 1934, Section 10, p. 1, published under the
title, 'Who is Then The Gentleman? A Few Notes on Sean O'Casey, The Irish
Dramatist, Who is Here With His Play *Within the Gates*'.

† American journalist and author. On the staff of the *New York Times*, from
1928 to his retirement in 1968. Assistant Drama Editor (1932–7) and Screen
Critic and Editor (1940–68).

1. 22 October, 1934. The play was directed by Melvyn Douglas.

for not convincing her of their desolation, apparently, and then dismissed them for luncheon. The morning rehearsal was ended.

*   *   *

Then, from the wings of the stage and as casual as one might please, there strolled a lean, raw-boned man of more than medium height. It was, of course, Mr O'Casey. He wore a shaggy, russet-coloured tweed suit, with a brown turtle-neck sweater under the jacket, and a cap of the same material pulled down at a haphazard angle over the left eye. His face was lean and ruddy, his nose long, and upon the bridge of it rested a pair of gold-rimmed spectacles with thick lenses, behind which were bright and penetrating eyes. One might have wished to ask him the score of the football match.

His complete informality was perfect—so perfect, in fact, that one liked him before a word was spoken. It was easy to perceive why this man, when he first went to London from Ireland's Abbey Theatre as a new dramatic 'lion', had refused to array himself in dress clothes for formal dinner parties. He was too obviously comfortable in the ones he was wearing. And when he did speak the richness of his Irish brogue and the low modulation of his voice were as warm as a Dublin snug.

*   *   *

The visitor admitted quite frankly that he had come on a somewhat impudent mission—to find out, in brief, what sort of man this playwright, O'Casey, is. A slow smile spread over his face.

'I've been married for seven years,' said he, 'and my wife doesn't yet know what sort of man I am.'

A friend, standing by, suggested that it takes eight tailors to make a man.

'Nine, isn't it?' corrected Mr O'Casey. 'But the Lord knows how many it takes to make an author!'

With the opportunity abandoned of seeing the author in immediate contact with his play—a play, incidentally, which has been hailed by drama critics who have read the script as a profound masterpiece—it was proposed that the visitor sit down with Mr O'Casey in an adjoining room for a chat. That was all right with the latter. Any place would do. And, there being only one chair in the room, he offered to sit on the floor. The contingency, however, was avoided.

*   *   *

The 'chat'—which eventually became a two-hour debate on most of the currently popular subjects and wove its way out of the theatre into a convenient tavern and back to the theatre again—was temporarily held up while an agent for the producers endeavoured to arrange a convenient time in which another visitor might see Mr O'Casey. A 'gentleman', the agent described him.

Mr O'Casey shot a sidelong glance from under the visor of his cap.

' "When Adam delve and Eve span, who was then the gentleman?" ' [2] he parried. 'Who *is* then the gentleman? I thought the only gentlemen were in England.'

The appointment was finally arranged, after considerable banter on the author's part—banter, the tenor of which was mostly an objection that no pretty women were ever brought around to interview him. Then the agent departed and the present visitor observed that Mr O'Casey seemed to enjoy his little joke.

'Did you think I was joking?' he innocently inquired. 'That's the funny thing—when an Irishman is serious people think he is joking, and when he jokes they think he's serious.'

His face assumed an expression of perturbation as the visitor asked whether Irishmen ever are serious.

'Serious! Man, I should say so! There's no more sincere people in the world than the Irish. Why, an Irishman would murder his own father or brother over a difference in creed or politics! If you want more evidence of sincerity than that, I don't know where you can find it.'

The conversation thereupon turned to a serious discussion of the theatre—after digressing hither and yon over one or two incidental subjects. The objection which Mr O'Casey has to the so-called realistic theatre was not long in manifesting itself, and the visitor, mindful of the celebrated debate which raged between the playwright and the Irish poet George Russell ('AE') over a matter of artistic standards,[3] was discreetly receptive.

*   *   *

He had seen several of Broadway's current attractions since his

2. English proverb attributed to John Ball, priest and agitator, who used it in a seditious speech at Blackheath before he was hanged in 1381.

3. 'Irish Literary Shillalahs', *New York Times*, 6 February, 1930, p. 22 [editorial on dispute between O'Casey and George Russell over art]. Provoked letter to the Editor from O'Casey (20 March, 1930).

arrival in New York—named those he could remember with a tone of distaste—but could say very little for any of them. The fashionable drawing-room comedy which invariably treats of sex was particularly open to his barbs.

'It may be a beautiful and useful thing to turn a stage into a drawing room,' said he, 'but to turn a drawing room into a stage is neither beautiful nor useful. The trouble is that these bloody men writing today don't know how to put one word to another. They have no vocabulary. There's not a line of poetry from one end of their plays to the other.'

But Shakespeare, Sheridan, Ibsen in some of his plays, Shaw—he named those and several others slowly, deliberately—ah, but they wrote poetry for the stage! To cite his point Mr O'Casey recited the opening lines from *King Richard III*—'Now is the winter of our discontent', etc. He rose from his chair, dropped his cap on a table, took a turn of the room and sat down again.

*   *   *

'Why should an author write for the stage in the way that people talk?' he asked. 'Is there anything beautiful in ordinary conversation —the sort of things that you and I are saying now? If I had the characters in my plays speak as Irishmen ordinarily speak, I'd be writing rubbish. *I get a copper phrase and do my best to turn it into gold.*'

The visitor inquired just when Mr O'Casey had begun writing plays. He was born in 1880, said he, 'so any one can compute how old I am now.' But when he began writing plays—well, that was no matter. It was necessary first to learn how to read and write, and that he had not had the opportunity to do until he was thirteen years old. Then he had taught himself. For many years he worked as a builder's labourer, dock hand and railway worker.

'And never in my life did I feel better than when I did physical labour," said he. "My chest measured 46, my arms were as big as tree limbs and I had a great ball of muscle here on my hand where I gripped the pickhandle. I weighed twelve stone twelve, and I worked all day and was ready to live joyously through the night.'

To Sean O'Casey, With Love*

LILLIAN GISH †

George Jean Nathan [1] considered Sean O'Casey and Eugene O'Neill the greatest playwrights in the world. George wrote a great deal about O'Casey and was disappointed when his play *Within the Gates* closed after a short run in London.[2] But he helped to bring the play over to the United States. I was grateful to George for doing this, although he was not responsible for my getting the role of the Young Whore in the production.

O'Casey came to this country for the rehearsals. During the first few months of production, he spent most of his time in my dressing room. 'I can't stay out there,' he would say, gesturing toward the lobby, his eyes twinkling behind their heavy glasses. 'They keep asking me what my play is about, and I don't know what to tell them.'

George arranged for him to stay at the Royalton Hotel, his own headquarters. O'Casey brought so few possessions—a few shirts, socks, and underwear—that he would put one sock in one drawer and its partner in another drawer. He seemed to own only the brown suit and cap that he wore. He spoke with an Irish lilt, and it was a joy to listen to the poetry in his speech. He was fascinated by electric gadgets, amazed by the different ways in which one could switch on a light—push, pull, twist, turn. He would go about, trying them all like a child.

His poetic turn of mind evidently appealed to our audiences, for the play ran in New York for six months. When we left to go on tour, word came to us in Philadelphia that the play had been banned in Boston. A short time later O'Casey wrote me:

---

* From *The Movies, Mr Griffith, and Me* (London: W. H. Allen; Englewood Cliffs, N.J.: Prentice-Hall, 1969), pp. 322–3.

† American film star of the silent days, and numerous other films since. From mid-twenties spent more time on the stage. Played part of the Young Whore in the New York production of *Within the Gates* (1934).

1. American drama critic (1882–1958).

2. The play, which opened at the Royalty Theatre, on 7 February, 1934, closed after 28 performances.

The last performance must have been a strange experience and I should have given a lot to be there, though not so much as I should have given to be present when the ban was declared in Boston. I got a whole pile of correspondence about it, and a lot of press-cuttings, but these couldn't give the thrill I'd have got from standing and hitting out in the centre of the fight.[3] Though the ban caused some excitement and a lot of talk, I should have preferred the tour and it is a pity that the Jesuits of Boston were able to stop it.

He added:

Let me thank you, Lillian, for a grand and a great performance; for your gentle patience throughout the rehearsals, and for the grand way you dived into the long and strenuous part of 'The Young Whore'.

The beautiful bound copy of *Within the Gates* that rests in my library has this inscription:

In Remembrance of Things Past,
of this play's production and performance
When we all, at least, battled
together for the return of some
of the great things that belong to Drama
A bad thing well done can never feel success;
A good thing well done can never feel failure.
                With love,
                        Sean O'Casey

3. Back in England, O'Casey did reply to his critics: *Blasts and Benedictions*, pp. 118–31.

Playwright and Box Office*

MAURICE BROWNE †

Browne: I know, Sean, that anyhow you are going to bruise my English head with your Irish heel, so, just to annoy you, I'll start by suggesting that the Theatre, the Playwright, and the Box Office are, as a matter of fact, whatever they should be in theory, the only possible ruling trinity in the theatrical world today with economic conditions as they are—I don't say as they should be or as you and I would have them in our pet private Utopia.

O'Casey: Believe you me, I don't want to go dreaming in any Utopian land: but I do want to walk in the region of common-sense. We can't have perfection yet, but we can become a little better than we are. It is an unholy trinity, with the box office controlling the theatre and modelling the playwright. The trinity of the theatre used to be the author, the actors, and the audience; but now it is the box office, the manager, and last, of course, the playwright, so that the theatre and drama not only do not come into the sun, but do not even come into the limelight. This devotion to the box office is not only making it more difficult for the English drama as a whole, it is also making it more difficult for the box office itself. Managers are now so eager to get a success that to win one they will rook the box office of every penny it possesses. The more eager they are for a success, the more difficult a success becomes because of the cost. When a play is written, the first thought is : What is it going to cost? The question of money, money is at the head and tail of it and in the very heart of all things connected with the putting on of a bad play or a good play. When a play's doing well, the box office is a haven of light and hilarity; when a play's doing badly, the box office is a place of desolation. So we see what a mill-stone round the neck of a manager the box office really is, for so much money is lavished even on a trivial play to make it into what is called a wow, that the very success desired

* BBC broadcast, published in *The Listener* (London), **20**, no. 495 (7 July, 1938), pp. 10–11. Reprinted in *Blasts and Benedictions*, ed. Ronald Ayling (London : Macmillan; New York : St Martin's Press, 1967), pp. 3–8.

† English dramatist, manager and actor (1881–1955), who produced R. C. Sherriff's play *Journey's End* in London for the first time, at the Savoy Theatre, on 21 January, 1929.

becomes the next thing to impossibility. And once a manager is unfortunate enough to make a pile out of some play, he immediately loses all he has gained by his frantic efforts to make a second pile.

Browne: Of course, you've got me when you talk about managers unfortunate enough to make a pile out of one play and idiots enough to lose it over others. I'm a bad case in point, as you know, you old rascal! But, joking apart, if you are going to buy a motor-car, or a wireless set, or a teething ring for the baby, isn't one of the very first questions you ask yourself: 'How much will it cost?' and the next question: 'Can I afford it?' I absolutely agree with you that the question of money is at the head and the tail of play production, but isn't the question of money also at the head and the tail of birth and death and every single and solitary thing in between? And do you really think that this fact has such a bad influence on the playwright?

O'Casey: A very bad influence indeed. Everything is against the playwright who thinks of his play, and everything in favour of the playwright who thinks of the box office; and woe unto him who does, for the playwright who thinks of the box office can never write a fine play.

Browne: Half-a-minute: what about Shakespeare, for example, or Euripides, or Chekhov, or Eugene O'Neill, or even one or two Irishmen I could mention—George Bernard Shaw for example, to say nothing of the author of *Juno and the Paycock*? Now, Sean, you just said 'The playwright who thinks of the box office can never write a fine play'. Can you give any real reason for saying that?

O'Casey: Of course I can. When a playwright thinks of the box office while he's writing a play, he's bound to try to model his play on the traditions with which the managers and actors are familiar. So, from the very start, he dare not write anything new. Anything new makes a play more difficult for the manager, more difficult for the actors, more difficult for the producer, and, most of all, more difficult for the poor box office. As for Shakespeare, his best works prove that while he was writing them, he couldn't have been dreaming of the box office. The length and power of the principal characters stand in the way of a long run, and without a long run there can be no success within the calculation of the box office. The parts of Hamlet, Othello, or Lear, are so huge and call for such tremendous effort that an actor playing any one of them for a year would kill the parts, and so kill the plays, or he would kill himself. The box office never dominated Shaw. He swept away the box office as he swept away the stupidities that littered the stage: but there are few playwrights with the fighting abilities of Shaw. We may have his courage, but courage may slay ourselves. Shaw's courage, so well directed, slew all who tried to slay him. O'Neill, if he ever thought of the box office, would never have written *Strange Interlude, The Great God Brown,* or *Mourning Becomes Electra.* No: managers and actors are still terrified of anything new. Tell us the old, old story, say the managers, so that the theatre may be made a place fit for box offices to live in! In a programme of a play running recently in the West End, the most important things mentioned are, not the play, not the actors, but a dress designed and made by Messrs Tweedledee, a hat designed and made by Messrs Tweedledoo, negligée and nightdress designed and made by Messrs Tweedledeedum, and glove, bags, and silverware designed and made by Messrs Tweedledumdee. The one thing forgotten on the programme was to mention that the author, the actors, and the audience were designed and made by God Almighty. Long ago, we used to go to see the play; later on we went to see the actors; now we go to see dresses, negligées, nightgowns, hats, gloves, and silverware. That's the kind of dramatic art we get since the box office has become the guardian angel of the English theatre.

Another sign of the evil effect of the box office: some time ago, in a kind of competition, a London management asked for plays. Before the sun could move from one solstice to another, the management were struggling with one thousand six hundred plays. Just think of it—not one thousand six hundred managements fighting over one play, but one management fighting with one thousand six hundred of them! What was the result? One thousand five hundred and ninety-nine good plays and one bad one? Hardly. Out of this mass of plays there were but two having a possible chance of production. Now this management wasn't one bossing a theatre like the Art Theatre of Moscow, or the Guild Theatre of New York, or the Abbey Theatre of Dublin, all ready to put on second-rate plays, at a pinch, but eager to get plays that would make a name for themselves, at home and abroad. No: the management that dealt with the one thousand six hundred plays wasn't so eager for world-wide fame as it was eager to secure a commercial success. And out of these one thousand six hundred plays this management got two that were possibly fit for production. We may safely assume that the writers of these plays had their eyes fixed fast on the box office. So we see that the box office has a bad effect even on those who concentrate on giving it honour and power. In fact, there are far more failures when the thoughts are of the box office, the whole box office, and nothing but the box office, than when it is completely banished from the mind of him who writes for the theatre.

Browne: Look here, Sean, I'm not defending the box office, but are you quite sure that you are thinking clearly? A moment ago you were talking of one thousand six hundred playwrights (yes, it's an awful thought, isn't it!) and you said that only two of them wrote plays that were possibly fit for production—good enough to sell to that management which had organised the competition. But how do you know that the management selected the two best plays? If it was half as bad a management as you suggest, it probably selected the two worst. And how do you know either that all those one thousand six hundred playwrights had their eyes fixed on the box office?

O'Casey: Well, mainly because the theatre is so constituted today that it is next to impossible for anyone writing for it to have his thoughts anywhere else. What is the art of the theatre of today but a hang-dog attachment to the law of supply and demand? Give the public what the playwrights and the managers think the public want—that is the law and the prophets in the theatre of today. The slogan of a great agency is, not 'You want the best plays—we have them', but 'You want the best seats—we have them'! And the law of giving what it is thought the public want is based on the box office. Only the other day a playwright who has had a box office success, is reported in a Sunday paper as saying: 'I think the public taste is for romantic plays with incidental music, a touch of probability, and characters taken from life'. So, I suppose, we should all strive to write romantic plays with incidental music till the taste of the public changes. 'The poets,' says Shelley, 'are the trumpets that call to battle; they are the unacknowledged legislators of the world.' Poor Shelley was wrong. Actually, it appears, the poets and playwrights are but the miserable camp-followers of what is thought to be the public taste. On the other hand, it may be he who searches out the public taste who is wrong! He tells us 'he thinks the public taste is such and such.' He thinks—he doesn't know. That's the thing that keeps them all hanging by the neck—the box office is never sure. Well, thank God, it's just as easy to have a sickening failure with a romantic play tricked out with incidental music as it is to have a financial failure with a play by Shakespeare, Shaw, Strindberg, or

O'Neill, or any other dramatist who thinks life is something more than a romantic glide, helped along by incidental music.

Browne: Bravo! I agree with every word you are saying now. Go on, rub it in.

O'Casey: Another sinister attraction of the box office is that when a playwright secures a financial success with any particular play (*Barretts of Wimpole Street,* for instance) many attempts are made by other playwrights to go and do likewise, and this imitation is encouraged and applauded by the managers on the strength of the idea that what is once done well can be done a dozen times badly. The managers have made imitation the curse of the theatre, as it is, to a greater degree, the curse of the films. How are we to bring about a change? Private energy and enterprise have sprinkled a little theatre here and there in England occasionally offering a chance of production to a new play by a new dramatist. But even these little theatres are continually struggling with financial difficulties. To do anything they must be nationally and municipally supported. The theatre in Shaftesbury Avenue must become the theatre of Islington, of Fulham, of Stepney, and so on, with the new National Theatre [1] leading the way in greater things for the glory of God and the honour of the English Theatre.

Browne: I'm not going to let you draw me off your trail with a controversial red herring like the National Theatre. But I *am* going to suggest that for those ills of our profession today which you denounce so rightly, the ultimate remedy isn't to be found in a National Theatre, and the ultimate fault doesn't lie in the managers, nor even in the box office. Surely both fault and remedy lie in ourselves. You've admitted the law of supply and demand. In Elizabethan days England demanded the best from its theatre and got it. Today we—the audience, the people—have grown lax in our demands; we let ourselves be fed with fifth-rate stuff at extravagant prices. But we can still get the best if we want it enough. And, if we want it enough, we'll demand it—and go on demanding it until we get it.

1. The National Theatre—his opinions on the subject can be found in both *The Flying Wasp* (1937) and *The Green Crow* (1956)—did not finally materialise until 1963.

Playwright in Exile*

RIA MOONEY †

I was in the Rathmines and Rathgar Musical Society in 1924 but I had never heard a word about him until after *Juno*. I never saw it until I joined the Abbey. Of course I had seen him many times, I mean I must have but I have no clear memory of him. The first time I recollect was the opening of *The Plough*. I remember him before it, his face was very animated and his eyes were all screwed up. Afterwards I met him. I was going home and you had to cross over the stage in those days to get out. Well the stage was empty and Sean was coming over from the other side and for the only time I saw that his face was white, expressionless, without any animation whatsoever. He stopped me and thanked me for the way I played Rosie. He said I saved his play. If the people had disliked Rosie the other two acts would have failed. He said I made them like her and I wondered how, and what he meant when he said that I saved his play.

During breaks we used to go into a lane at the back of the Abbey and I used to see country girls out there, about fifteen years of age or so and they used always to be with soldiers. They had glittering eyes and white faces with red rings of crimson paint on their cheeks. I commented on them to someone and I was told that they were prostitutes. And I felt so sorry for them that when the Covey called me a prostitute I was hurt, hurt on their behalf. I must have conveyed this feeling to the audience and I got sympathy from them. That I suppose is what he meant when he said that I saved his play.

Thursday night was the night the riots started. I can remember well a young man with black hair in the stalls (I often wonder who he was), and he was waving his fist at me and telling me to get off the stage, that I was a disgrace to my sex, my religion and my country.

You know that they tried to kidnap Barry Fitzgerald, Shelah Richards and myself. Someone came knocking at our door but I

---

* Sean McCann (ed.), *The World of Sean O'Casey* (London: The New English Library, Four Square Books, 1966), pp. 167–70.

† Abbey actress, who played the part of Rosie Redmond, the Prostitute, in the 1926 production of *The Plough and the Stars*. Later directed for the Abbey Theatre. She also directed the London production of *Red Roses for Me* at the Embassy Theatre in 1946.

wouldn't let my father open the door and let them in. We had to go to the Theatre every other night by car. During my act the lights would be put on in the auditorium and the walls were lined with detectives. They threw pieces of coal, pennies, anything they had. Some nights later they used stink bombs.

My school friends cut me for playing in it. Some people, friends of mine, came to me and asked me if I was going to play that horrible character. They said that I should tell my father confessor. Of course I had no intention of telling my father confessor, but before the first night I mentioned it to a priest, but he only laughed and said 'Aren't you an actress?'

When the curtain came down the riots began. Some woman tried to set fire to the curtain and it was raised. Several climbed up on the stage and I still can see Barry Fitzgerald in fisticuffs with a man who had climbed up.

One distinguished actor [1] dissociated himself from O'Casey's plays and I think that Sean never forgave him.

One day there was a matinée, so instead of going home we all stayed on for tea. During the interval we had tea in the green-room and Gort cake. Rummel, the well-known pianist, came along with Lady Gregory and he played for us. That was the only time I ever spoke to Lady Gregory. She put her hand on my shoulder and said 'You've done well, very well, little girl'.

At that time there was a meeting of Cumann na mBan [2] and Sean was asked to defend his play. Shelah Richards, Gabriel Fallon, Barry Fitzgerald, Frank Hugh O'Donnell, Lyle Donaghy (the poet in whom Yeats was very interested) and myself all went along with Sean to support him. It was the first time I heard Maud Gonne [3] speak. She attacked his plays and mentioned Mary Bentham and her child.

Well when Sean went up to defend himself he could hardly speak as his eyes were very sore from the lights, and he asked if he could wear his cap to protect his eyes from the glare. He put it on but it didn't do any good for he still couldn't continue. One felt very sorry for him. The whole thing turned out to be a fiasco. He couldn't defend himself.

I met him in London at the time he was writing *The Tassie* and

1. Peter Judge (F. J. McCormick).
2. The women's auxiliary branch of the Volunteers.
3. Renowned Nationalist leader.

he told me that he had spent three weeks trying to write the Corporal's speech. He liked to go amongst the workers at the time and talk to them but he had to give it up because they tipped their caps to him and called him Sir. He didn't like that and I often wonder if that was why he dressed rather shabbily afterwards.

I asked him why he didn't live in Dublin and he told me that he never would because the people were so horrid to him.

I never knew a Sean O'Casey who wasn't kind, gentle and sensitive. But he wasn't shy. He'd come into the green-room after a performance and if he thought so he'd say that we were bloody awful, which, of course, didn't endear him to a lot of people.

At the time I was going to direct *Red Roses for Me* he was living in England. I wrote to him about production and he'd write back, sometimes contradicting what he had written in a previous letter. We had a vitriolic correspondence and you know it wasn't too safe at the time to be getting letters from Totnes with a stamp on the back which said 'Friends of the Soviet Union'.

Well we seemed to be getting nowhere and Sir Bronson Albery [4] suggested that I go over and stay with him for a while, for five minutes' conversation would be a lot better than all the correspondence.

When I arrived, Eileen and that lovely son of theirs, Niall, who died later, met me and they were so friendly. There was an intangible middle-class Dublin atmosphere about the house. When we were going in to have high tea Sean joined us, I think he had been writing in the study. I was very glad to see him and I think that he felt so and everything was forgotten.

I was after reading *Drums Under the Windows* and I mentioned it to him and how I found that the tempo increased as it went on. Towards the end the writing becomes so rapid that I found it hard to read it, it was so fast. Well we talked about it and his writing and he said to me, and it was only then that he mentioned those vitriolic letters, 'When I take a pen into my hand something comes over me and I can't help being bitter, even when I write letters.' [5]

4. London Theatre Manager who staged *Red Roses for Me* in 1946.
5. Once, when Alan Dent accompanied Brooks Atkinson on one of his regular visits to O'Casey when he later moved to Torquay, O'Casey remarked that it was the first time a British critic had called, though New York ones came regularly. When Dent pointed out that O'Casey had attacked English critics, O'Casey said with a smile, '*Sure, they should have the sense to know that I'm only venomous when I have a pen in me hand.*' In himself, though, he wasn't

bitter, as many outsiders seem to imply. R. M. Fox, in *The World of Sean O'Casey*, p. 49, writes: 'With all his bitterness, Sean O'Casey remained a very likeable man. I met his wife when she came to Dublin to see the production of *The Bishop's Bonfire* (1955). . . . She is a woman of discernment and of charm. I asked her, "Is Sean as bitter as ever?" She looked at me in amazement. "How can a man with a soft voice like that, be bitter?"'

Red Roses for Sean*

EILEEN O'CASEY †

Red Roses for Me, published in 1942, was written when we lived in Totnes—a very old and attractive town on the River Dart in Devon.

Every Friday, a market was held in the market-square of this town. Sean came to the market with me each week and, indeed, looked forward to it with great joy. The place was a hive of activity: farmers from the surrounding villages brought in their produce to be auctioned, and we housewives would bid for the lots of eggs, butter, etc., and afterwards share them out among ourselves. This was before the second world war—what a shame these market-scenes are all gone from Totnes now!

Regularly each Friday, an old man came to this market, not to buy, just to walk about and chat. He buttonholed Sean each week, pouring out his troubles to him. His constant worry was his money in the bank, whether the bank was safe. Weekdays must have been a torment to him, because each day of the week he must have realised the bank clerks were working hard to keep his money safe. He also had a few stocks and shares. This must have meant a daily scanning of the paper. He had a small house which he owned, and was in a constant state in case the woman who cleaned it was robbing him. He also owned a small cottage and, wet or fine, went to collect the rent each week, always in terror, in case it would not be paid the following week.

He was a strange and wonderful old character and I noticed Sean

* Programme note for the production of *Red Roses for Me*, at the Lyric Players Theatre, Belfast, in March 1972. The play was directed by Mary McCracken.

† Widow of the playwright, who wrote a memoir of her husband, entitled *Sean* (London: Macmillan, 1971; New York: Coward, McCann and Geoghegan, 1972; reprinted London: Pan Books, 1973).

jotting down notes when chatting with him. 'I am putting that old man into my new play, Eileen,' he said to me one day, and that is how 'Brennan o' the Moor' came to life.

The character of Brennan o' the Moor was also partly derived from an old man in Dublin who used to play the fiddle in the streets.

Mrs Breydon, surely, is Sean's mother, who had an influence on him all his life. Sean said and wrote many wonderful things about her. He writes in the chapter of his autobiography entitled 'Mrs Casside takes a Holiday': 'Life would be chill for him, when that warm heart had ceased to beat. . . . If ever a woman in this world had earned a rest from her labours, this was the one. He didn't wish her to live because of any pleasure death might take away from her. He wished it simply because she seemed to make life easier for him. Nay, not seemed; she did. To wish her to live was a great weakness which he couldn't shake aside. He was the one of her children who had been with her all the time. Thirty-five years or so she had cared for, and defended, him. Her works would follow her. What works? Attending to him! That wouldn't fetch her even a good-conduct medal from a local G. H. Q. of heaven! This woman's spiritual hardihood, her unshakable energy, her fine intelligence had all been burned to unusable ashes in the tedious smokiness of a hapless life. Life had wasted all her fine possessions. None, save he, could recognise her for what she was; and he was powerless to yield her any words of praise, for if he spoke them, there were none to hear. She would die alone—unhonoured and unsung.'

Sean's mother was not unhonoured. She was honoured in his writings and in his plays; all who read Sean's work will know how brave and noble a character she was. Ayamonn portrays slightly Sean himself, his writings, his activities in his young days, his brothers' love of theatre. All is told in his autobiographies. Sheila is the girl who loved Ayamonn, but was frightened by his poverty and his wild ideas of religion and class. She could be any young girl incapable of standing by her love and unable to fight against her own upbringing. Finnoola, especially, is poignant in her beauty with her dreams, which Sean's imagination has conjured up, bringing great beauty, gaiety and joy to his life for just a short while, with all ugliness gone. Because life has not yet marred her grace, charm, and beauty this makes it overwhelming, as one knows what life and poverty can do to the Finnoolas of this world. The Rev. E. Clinton is based on Sean's friend the Rev. E. M. Griffin, Protestant rector, a man Sean consciously or unconsciously puts into a good many of his writings. He had a great regard and affection for this man.

In the *Bridge* scene, his great love of Ireland is shown, his impatience, grief and scorn at the waste of such fine people.

The one single shilling is a symbol of what so many strikes and riots are all about. It represents the ideal we all have in mind, doing away with injustice, poverty, hunger. As the play stresses, '*Maybe he saw the shilling in th' shape of a new world*'.

Two Glimpses of O'Casey*

DOM WULSTAN PHILLIPSON, O.S.B.

I was among the audience, in a pit seat(price 1s. 3d., at the first performance of *Juno and the Paycock* at the Abbey Theatre on 3 March, 1924, and realised that this was one of the great moments of my life which had been devoted to the theatre ever since my mother took me, aged seven, to my first play, *John Bull's Other Island*,[1] by George Bernard Shaw, at the same theatre. Forty years after, my impressions of F. J. McCormick as Joxer, Barry Fitzgerald as the Paycock and Sara Allgood as Juno are still fresh in the memory: truly they were giants in the Abbey Theatre in those days. One memory of that evening, however, is still more vivid: the audience, realising that it had been present at the birth of a masterpiece which left it in that high state of exaltation between triumph and tears which great tragedy superbly played can always evoke, clamoured for the author. An enormous man with piercing eyes behind enormously thick glasses, dressed like a Dublin navvy in shabby raincoat, and carrying a cloth cap, came shyly upon the stage, thanked Lady Gregory, 'the charwoman of the Abbey', for her kindness towards him, and thanked the audience for their wonderful reception of his play. He received an ovation.

A short time before, I had been accepted for the Abbey Players by Michael Dolan during his term as actor-manager, but I had left Dublin for Downside when my chit for rehearsal came. Michael, one

---

* *Westminster Cathedral Chronicle* (London), **59**, no. 3 (March 1965), p. 46.

1. First staged at the Abbey Theatre on 25 September, 1916.

of the finest of the older Abbey Players, said to me when he heard that I had gone to Downside as a monk instead: 'Never mind, Father, the other Abbey will look after you much better than we could here in this one'.

I never thought that I should ever see Sean O'Casey again, although his works had become very familiar to me. Then I went to spend a few days with an old Dublin friend, Father Edwin Russell, at Totnes. He had tried to call on O'Casey and had not been well received; but I was determined to try my luck, so I went to his unpretentious little house and, in some trepidation, knocked at the door. It was opened by Breon O'Casey, a well-built dark boy of about seventeen, who received me courteously and went to ask his father if he would like to meet a Dubliner who was a great lover of his plays. I was immediately shown into the living-room and O'Casey rose to greet me with outstretched hand and welcoming smile.

He was about seventy years of age and the face showed traces of the suffering that had so long been his. Born in the slums on the North side of Dublin, he was not strong and his sight was very weak: he had known penury and hunger, which had given him a prophet-like austerity of countenance, but in the eyes there was a mischievous kindly twinkle which he shared with his fellow Dubliners and friends, Shaw and Brendan Behan. We talked affectionately of F. J. McCormick, Barry Fitzgerald, Michael Dolan and Sara Allgood. He agreed with me that 'F.J.' was perhaps the greatest of all the Abbey players, and asked me for news of 'F.J.'s' widow, Eileen Crowe, and her children, whom I had seen a short while before. We talked of Michael Dolan's brilliant performance in *Autumn Fire* by T. C. Murray and of Lennox Robinson and about his acting in *Henry IV* by Pirandello with the Dublin Drama League. Then, like James Joyce, we talked of all the familiar Dublin streets and squares —Fitzwilliam Street, Merrion Square, Thomas Street, Henry Street, Moore Street and O'Connell Street. We talked of Lady Gregory, Yeats and Pearse, whom he loved and admired, and to whom he paid generous tribute in *Drums Under the Windows*. We talked for about two hours.

Breon was despatched to get us tea and biscuits after about an hour's talk and it seemed strange to be drinking tea with one who was supposed to be both anti-clerical and anti-Catholic. The fact is that Sean O'Casey was so full of the milk of human kindness that the individual could be sure of a welcome if the 'general' had to endure the lash of his satire. I did not altogether escape. 'Would you ever come to talk informally to some Downside boys in my room in the school?' I asked him. With the twinkle in his eye he said, 'Father, if I am ever in the Bath direction I'll gladly come and talk to yourself for as long as you like. I've enjoyed our gossip about old days and old people in Dublin and the Abbey. But I won't talk to your boys, whatever you say, for you might not like what I'd tell them.' A great playwright, a great fighter, a great lover; his memory will endure like that of Yeats, Synge and Shaw in the Dublin he loved.

Uninvited Guest*

ALLAN CHAPPELOW †

It was with some trepidation that I rang the front door-bell of Sean O'Casey's home at Totnes, in South Devon. I had long cherished a wish to meet this great man, and, perhaps, also be granted a sitting, photography being my chief hobby.

The door was opened by his son Breon, who entertained me until he could broach the matter with his father, who was asleep at the time. Breon is a painter. He had studied in Paris and London. We discussed two paintings by Augustus John which were hanging in the room. One, I learnt, had been the artist's wedding gift to the writer.

Then the door burst open and the great man strode in on our conversation, hand outstretched, and smiling broadly.

'Well, now—what is it you're wanting of me?' were his first words.

'I want to take a photograph of you as I did of Bernard Shaw, the Webbs, H. G. Wells and Augustus John,' I replied boldly.

'Oh, indeed, and do you, now; all these people you've been running around taking photographs of—it takes up a lot of time?' he remarked quizzically.

---

* Extracted from *Times Pictorial* (Dublin) [formerly *Weekly Irish Times*], 78, no. 4,116, 13 September, 1952, p. 14; originally entitled 'Appointment with Sean O'Casey'.

† Author and journalist. Student of London University, when he visited and photographed O'Casey. Author of *Shaw, The Villager and Human Being* (London, 1961), and *Shaw—'The Chucker-Out'* (London, 1969).

'Oh, but I enjoy it—photography is my chief hobby,' I parried.

'Och—I didn't mean *your* time—I meant *theirs*,' was his genial rejoinder!

*   *   *

We got on to the subject of education.

'The only way to learn or to be any good at anything is to be interested in it and educate yourself,' was O'Casey's emphatic opinion, and he went on to tell me—quite without bitterness—of how his own education had been in the streets of Dublin. 'I don't suppose I had more than one year's proper schooling, all in all,' he added.

'Children must feel free to follow their interest, and not feel under any obligation to the parents. I've always treated my children as equals, and not expected anything back from them. I don't meddle. I'm of a different generation—what right should I have to meddle? Fledglings flee the nest in their own good time—the debt contracted to one's parents in one's youth is paid to one's offspring. That is the natural order of things.'

I asked him his views on co-education.

'Well—there's something to be said on both sides there,' he replied. 'I think it's a good thing for the sexes to mix after lessons are over, but not during them, or at too early an age. It then only upsets them —they can't concentrate.' O'Casey tipped back his chair, drew a long puff at his pipe, and pushed his wide-brimmed sombrero hat back on his head. 'Well, you'd better take that photograph, young man,' he then said, smiling broadly.

I did—about sixteen in all. O'Casey was a most co-operative and helpful sitter.

*   *   *

When I had finished he invited me to stay for a meal. Here was one of the most charming and exciting characteristics of the Irishman. I had come with diffidence to ask the privilege of a five-minute sitting; I had talked with him for some hours and now I was to sup with him.

I was then treated to a discourse on Russia and Communism. O'Casey considered that our only hope was for people to feel a sense of duty and fulfilment in working for the benefit of the community as a whole, and that this ideal could never be realised under capitalism. He pointed out that this need not conflict with the individual's desire for creative self-expression, and described how in Russia every factory had comprehensive libraries and facilities for study and recreation after working hours—which few or none in Britain had—and were encouraged to develop this side of their nature side by side with their work. He thought England had become a hopeless country for the artist. . . .

'Women should have some expression of their own individuality, but it's terribly difficult for women these days. It's so difficult to make both ends meet for most families and most women have to do a lot of housework themselves. We have three children [1] ourselves and I know what a full-time job bringing up children is to the mother of the family.'

*   *   *

It was now getting late and the great man moved from his chair. We shook hands warmly at the gateway, I feeling strongly that his heart was very much in the right place, and that I had had a most enviable and memorable experience with one of the really great dramatists of all time.

How Irish of the man! I had expected only ten minutes and he had given me hours! No wonder his opening remark had been: 'All this time it takes—no, not yours—theirs'!

1. Breon (b. 1928), Niall (1936–56; died of leukaemia), Shivaun (b. 1939).

The Rebel who Never Retired*

LAURENCE THOMPSON †

The taxi-driver, who came from Lancashire, thought that Torquay had recently seen a play by its most distinguished inhabitant, but he wasn't sure.

Mr Rattigan's Aunt Edna, who must form a good proportion of

* *News Chronicle* (London), 3 March, 1955, p. 6. Also included in *Irish Digest* (Dublin), 53, no. 3 (May 1955), pp. 8–10. Extracts from this interview appeared in *Evening Herald* (Dublin), 5 March, 1955, under the title of 'Melodrama Defended'.

† English journalist and author.

Torquay's winter population, would scarcely feel at ease with O'Casey. And O'Casey, in the drawing-room of his airy flat above the town, among the kind of furniture which is pictured in *Homes and Gardens*, and sold by Heal's, seemed little more congruous.

He wore brown corduroy jacket, hard-wearing trousers, new suede wool-lined ankle slippers, the famous brand of turtle-necked sweater which he bore through the United States as Wilde bore his lily.

Wisps and tufts of thin grey hair escaped like dangerous thoughts from the respectable durance of a blue cloth skull-cap, patterned in sky-blue, cerise and yellow.

With his long, inquisitive nose and red, dim eyes behind steel-rimmed spetctacles, he looked now like a leprechaun, now like an old priest by Anatole France, but mostly like a child of the Dublin tenements who has come to glory but isn't sure where to knock out his pipe.

The John portrait on the wall pinned him exactly; deliberately drab and proletarian, snuggling into anonymity lest Authority pick on him for something, giving himself away only by the crimson handkerchief cascading from his breast pocket like a ribald splash of laughter.

*   *   *

His talk wanders round the firmament, from James Joyce to the Elizabethan English spoken in the Dublin of his youth, from the colour bar to the cobalt bomb, full of crackling phrases—'You've got to believe in God, if you don't believe in Man'—and self-revealing parentheses—of St Paul, 'I don't give a damn what a man says, or what he believes, or what he thinks, as long as he writes well.'

He sees the great world with the disconcerting topsy-turvy wonder of a child: '*The Times*, now, that must be a pretty important newspaper'; and 'You're from London? There must be an awful lot of London men in the world; the birthrate of that city must be tremendous.'

Surprisingly, after the petty prickliness of *Sunset and Evening Star*, he is tolerant: 'Poor old Churchill, he doesn't seem very hopeful. He sees Russia as the enemy. I suppose it's the only possible view to take from his point of view.'

And looking back to the troubled times without which there would have been no *Plough and Stars*, he salutes the English as chivalrous, if often stupid opponents: 'The Tommies were always welcome when they came to search. One came to search my room. When he was out of sight of his officer, he let his rifle butt fall on the ground, lit a cigarette and said'—O'Casey imitates, not quite correctly, the Cockney whine; he has never been entirely at his ease outside Ireland —' "You haven't anything in here, have you?"

'It was damn cold that winter. Before he sent me outside, the officer said, "Haven't you got an overcoat? You'd better put it on, then." He needn't have done, you know.'

* * *

O'Casey insists that he is a Communist. 'But I'm not a Communist pamphlet. There are a whole lot running around who are no more than Communist pamphlets.'

And Soviet art is dry-as-dust, out-of-date. 'I tell them, "You honour Tolstoy and Chekhov, but you'll never have another if you don't be brave." '

He recalls how, when Stalin died, Picasso did a child's vision of the dead hero for a French paper, which some bureaucrat condemned.

The long, sensitive forefinger stabs the air, and the voice becomes more astringently, defiantly Dublin : 'If I'd been editor of that paper, I'd have written to that Soviet official and said, "Go to HELL"!'

Then a little later there is a parenthesis—'Anarchism is a higher form than Communism'—and a statement of faith, 'I'm against any system which doesn't allow every man and every woman the admission to all the gifts of the universe.'

That, really, is what the plays have been about. That is why it is right to call O'Casey, the agnostic, a religious man, and *The Bishop's Bonfire* a religious play.

* * *

'It's the spirit of a book written by our own Catholic clergyman, Dr Walter McDonald,[1] who was forty years a professor of theology at Maynooth. He wanted theology to advance like any other science. I hope this play may do something.

'The whole play's symbolical. The critics say that I spoil the last act with melodrama. But the shooting's symbolical. If that hadn't

1. To whom O'Casey dedicated *Inishfallen, Fare Thee Well*, as well as, in part, *The Drums of Father Ned*. McDonald was a theologian of fiercely independent views, whose *Reminiscences of a Maynooth Professor* (London, 1925) made a deep impression on O'Casey.

been done, if it had ended with Keelin's man going away, that would have meant death just the same, a life of frustration and despair.'

And that, to the old revolutionary, is a symbol of Ireland, the world.

Besides—the Old Micky peeps slyly out—'I'm still interested in melodrama. I don't see why there shouldn't be a little bit of melodrama. It's a play, you see, the theatre's make-believe.'

Will London see the latest play [2] of the greatest playwright writing in English? He awaits news. London has not been overkind to him. Ninety-nine per cent of his income is from America, and that from the autobiographies rather than plays.

'They've sold not well, you know, but they've kept me from penury. I keep a family of six, you know, and everything's sliced by 9s. in the pound. But I've no reason to complain. If I didn't work, what the hell would I do? I'm a naturally lazy fellow.'

*   *   *

Best of all, perhaps, would be if his own country honoured its own prophet.

'My nearer love is with the Irish people.' A pause and the quick, thin smile that is never far from his lips. 'But they don't seem to appreciate me very much.'

As I left, he was telling me how to bring up my children, whom he has not seen, as if, like the rest of humanity, they belonged to him.

A great man, and a good one. The two don't go together all that often.

2. *The Bishop's Bonfire* was first performed in Dublin, at the Gaiety Theatre, on 28 February, 1955. Its London première was to follow later, in 1961, at the Mermaid Theatre.

Visiting Sean O'Casey in Devon*

BORIS IZAKOV †

Sean O'Casey's life has much in common with Gorky's. He began as a manual worker, and he has Gorky's love of humanity. O'Casey has a very young, boyish smile—just like Bernard Shaw (another famous Irishman), with whom he had for many years a close friendship.

O'Casey is a fascinating conversationalist, and loves an argument. During a heated discussion, he bends his head to one side and leans forward, and looks rather like a big, angry bird.

Our conversation turned to the question why his plays are not staged in Soviet theatres, although the author of them is so close to us 'in spirit'.

I told him that the Soviet citizen has a warm regard for every national liberation movement and for those who belong to them, but in O'Casey's plays the ordinary Irish people, many of whom are shown in the struggle for their country's independence, are depicted, in my opinion, with too great a realism; frequently, his principal characters are unattractive, unheroic. Could the Soviet theatre reconcile itself to something so contradictory? All this I expressed as best I could to O'Casey, mentioning, of course, that this was my own personal opinion.

O'Casey objected:

'I don't at all find my main characters unattractive. They are the product of existing conditions in my country. I like them just as they are. Social conditions will change and they will become more sympathetic. But, in the meanwhile, they cannot turn into the model men and women that you desire them to be. You must not expect

---

* Extracted from *Sovetskaya Kultura* (Moscow), 15 December, 1955, no. 153, p. 4. The original was part of a feature article, entitled 'Five Meetings' [interviews with Bertrand Russell, James Aldridge, Sean O'Casey, Howard Fast and Lion Feuchtwanger].

† Author and translator. Friend of O'Casey who corresponded regularly with him. (Eileen O'Casey, *Sean*, p. 274.)

from my "heroes" what you expect from characters in Soviet literature—the literature of a different society.'[1]

1. O'Casey's anti-heroism is an uncompromising feature of his plays—his
early plays especially. In *The Plough and the Stars*, his 'heroes' are beloved
cowards, spending much of their time laughing and looting. ('Joxer', in *Juno
and the Paycock*, remarks, significantly, '*It's better to be a coward than a
corpse!*') Even in *The Bishop's Bonfire*, the character of Codger Sleehaun can
best be described as a very likeable old rogue, who makes the most of his
opportunities and contributes largely to the play's audacious fun and knock-
about farce.

Talking to Sean O'Casey on American Television*

ROBERT EMMETT GINNA †

This interview was filmed at O'Casey's home in Torquay

Ginna: Visiting you here brings up a question that puzzles a great
many people and that is why it has been that Ireland has sent forth
so many of her sons, her great writers, to make their living away
from Ireland, starting way back in the eighteenth century with
Goldsmith and Sheridan, and then on down to Shaw and Joyce.

O'Casey: Well, of course, Bob, that's a big question—a question
that very few can answer and I don't happen to be one of the few.
For instance, I couldn't tell you why Goldsmith or Sheridan left. I'm
not that old yet. But the question of Shaw and the question of the
other writers that so frequently and sometimes so hastily leave Ireland
is a complex question. It arises for many reasons, but one of the big
reasons is, of course, that London and New York unfortunately are
of far greater importance than Dublin.

* A shortened transcript of the National Broadcasting Company's filmed interview, 'A Conversation with Sean O'Casey and Robert Emmett Ginna', in the
'Elder Wise Men' series, shown on American TV, 22 January, 1956. The film
was directed by Robert D. Graff.
 † American film producer, who also collaborated with Graff in the production of the John Ford film for Metro-Goldwyn-Mayer of O'Casey's early life-
story—based on the playwright's autobiographies—*Young Cassidy* (1965).

Ginna: Well, now, tell me, in your own case, after you left Ireland, how was it you came to settle here in Devon?

O'Casey: Well, in one sense, I don't believe I can settle anywhere. Probably I won't even be able to settle serenely in Heaven if I get there. But the real reason for coming to Devon was that we were anxious about the education of our children. I knew nothing about the subject because it was a thing I'd no experience of. I never went to school and, of course, I never went to college. I saw the gates and passed by the gates of Trinity College several times in the day, but I never went inside of them. So I left that question entirely to Eileen and she naturally went and asked Shaw's advice, and Shaw immediately said, 'Dartington Hall, Eileen, that's the place for the O'Casey children—one of the best schools in England. Send them there.' So she, acting on Shaw's advice, decided to send them to Dartington Hall School. The two of us were against separation from our children. We didn't want them to live in, board in, so we decided then to get a place as close as possible to the school, so that the children could come home every night. Or, if they did eventually become boarders, as two of them did, they could at least come home at the week-end and continue to enjoy the communion of family life. I'm very glad indeed that we did choose Devon, because Devon is a delightful county and the Devon people are a charming community.

Ginna: The great playwrights whom you admire, who particularly inspire you—Shakespeare, Ibsen, Eugene O'Neill—their plays all have some common quality, though, that makes them general, not particular; makes them reach out to all humanity. What do you think there is in a play that does that?

O'Casey: Well, they reach out to all humanity because they all are human, you see. O'Neill and Shakespeare and the other ones that you quoted, are full of emotion and life and they react to this and they put this emotion into a play. It's the same thing that happens to everybody: life and death and birth and sorrows and sadness and joy, or a keen or a wailing or a lament over a dead person and a song over people that have been newly married.

Ginna: Shakespeare's characters are no different from O'Casey's characters, then?

O'Casey: Take the character of Falstaff. I've often heard critics talk about characters in an English play: they were as large as life, they were matter-of-fact characters, they were as if you'd brought people out of the street and planted them down in the centre of the stage. No sir, you couldn't do that. There's no character in the whole history of the drama that's more realistic from their point of view or as large as life as the character of Falstaff. But Falstaff *isn't* a matter-of-fact character. You couldn't go out into the street and bring in a Falstaff and put him on to the stage because there's no Falstaff existing out in the street. Falstaff is far larger than life and, of course, Shakespeare knew this. God, if you like, created Shakespeare, but it was Shakespeare that created Falstaff.

Ginna: But tell me, now, after these many years, what have you found out about life? What do you really believe now?

O'Casey: That's a big question. But what is life? Ah, well, that's a question similar to the one that 'Captain' Boyle put to 'Joxer', you know: *'What is the stars, Joxer? What is the stars? That's the question!'* 'What is life, Bob, what is life?' Well, I have found life *an enjoyable, enchanting active and sometimes a terrifying experience*; and I've enjoyed it completely. *A lament in one ear, maybe; but always a song in the other.* And to me life is simply an invitation to live. . . .

'It Was Fun,' said Sean O'Casey*

JOSEPH STEIN †

In July, 1956, my wife and I made the four-hour train trip from London to the seashore town of Torquay, in Devon, to keep an appointment with Sean O'Casey. The appointment had been arranged before we left New York, and I was meeting the great playwright to discuss with him adapting his *Juno and the Paycock* as a musical.

There had been some preliminary correspondence with O'Casey before the trip, but the project was too important and complicated to be settled by mail. And so, we went to Torquay.

* Extracted from *Irish Digest* (Dublin), 45, no. 3, May, 1959, pp. 50–2.

† Librettist who adapted *Juno and the Paycock* into a musical comedy. The success of *Juno*, as a musical, was short-lived, running for less than a month. It was staged at New York's Winter Garden Theatre in March, 1959.

I remember my first reaction as he greeted us. He seemed so fragile and delicate, spoke so softly, that for a moment I regretted that we had come. I felt we were imposing ourselves on him, forcing him to entertain two strangers, and that it was a physical effort for him.

In a few minutes I saw I was wrong. Mr O'Casey may be physically worn (he was then recovering from an illness), but he is so full of bubble and spirit, so curious about and delighted with people, that very shortly he had us chatting and laughing like old friends.

As we talked of a musical version of *Juno*, O'Casey told us frankly that he was not familiar with the musical form, as it had been developed in America. He knew of some of the Rodgers and Hammerstein works, of course, and about *My Fair Lady*, but he had not seen any of them on the stage. (I had brought the cast album of *My Fair Lady*, only to find that the O'Caseys had no phonograph.)

As I discussed the musical form and outlined how I thought *Juno* could be transformed into a musical, O'Casey warmed to the idea very quickly. We talked about the projected outline I had prepared, and he was delighted with the sense of telling the story of the Boyles in more varied locales, and with song and dance. I sketched the position of several scenes, with suggested songs, and O'Casey started to visualise the larger stage, the fuller canvas.

Every once in a while he turned to his wife and mine for comment, and as the discussion continued, the whole idea of the musical, which had seemed so vague to him, seemed to take distinct and concrete shape in his mind. I had the feeling that he saw it . . . new scenes, songs, chorus and all . . . come to life on the stage.

*   *   *

We talked of many things: the plays appearing at the time in London and on Broadway; the changes in the American scene since his last visit; he was interested in the growth of suburbia, in the American political climate; he reminisced about the Abbey Theatre, about his friendship with Shaw, about his experiences during the bombings.

He asked about our children, not with polite curiosity but with real interest, and his deep love for children shone through his questions. 'They have a right to a large life,' he said at one point, 'without boundaries.'

The O'Caseys had moved to Devon, he told us, when their children were young, because there were good schools nearby and the children could live at home. This is not too common in England. 'The English like to hide their children,' he said.

As we were leaving, I said that I had felt honoured to have met with him. He did not approve of the word. 'It was fun,' he said. 'That's the word. It was fun.'

When we left Torquay, it was with his approval of the musical project, and with his blessings.

*　　*　　*

In our correspondence during the work on the musical, O'Casey was encouraging and helpful and always modest. He pointed out that he had no experience with the musical form, once adding, 'I wish I had, for playwrights should be well up in all forms done in the theatre; but circumstances forced me to begin late, and I had no time, no time, no time. . . .' But he felt, as we described by mail what was being done, that we were being true to the spirit and feeling of the original.

*　　*　　*

Our conversation was interrupted once by the arrival of O'Casey's doctor, who was an old friend.

When the doctor asked him how he felt, O'Casey, in a wonderfully pixie way, threw himself on the doctor's chest and wailed like a baby: 'I'm a sick man, doctor, a sick man.'

The doctor was delighted to see him in such high spirits.

Talk with a Titan*

PAUL SHYRE †

I spent two weeks visiting Sean O'Casey—a Titan of the theatre—
at his home in Torquay, a beautiful resort on the Devon coast.

We drove through town a short way to St Marychurch, around
Trumlands Road, and then through the large gateway, where Sean
was sitting in the garden on a beach chair waiting for me.

There he was, the Green Crow himself, watching me through his
spectacles, in his thick white turtle-neck pullover, and a beanie on his
head designed with bananas and oranges, his long hair hanging
beneath it.

We then discussed Dublin and my visit there. He referred to it as
'a city of silvered cynicism'. I told him I visited many spots where
he had lived, especially the small house in Abercorn Road, at no. 18,
where he lived with his mother until her death.

'It's still there, isn't it? We lived upstairs with very small space
for our own use. When I tried to write up there, there was a great
deal of noise, the walls were so thin. But I soon got used to all that.
If you really want to write something, you'll do it, bad conditions
or not.'

---

* Condensed version of the article, 'Talk with Two Titans' [Sean O'Casey
and Edward Gordon Craig], which appeared in *New York Times*, 8 September, 1957, Section 2, pp. 1, 3.

† American theatre director and adapter. Produced dramatised versions of
O'Casey's autobiographies in New York, from 1957 onwards—*I Knock at the
Door*, and, later, *Pictures in the Hallway*. Co-directed, with Philip Burton, the
successful Broadway production of *Purple Dust*, 1956–7, and, in 1958, *Cock-
a-Doodle Dandy*.

O'Casey Out to Make them Laugh*

DONAL FOLEY †

Sean O'Casey was at work on a new play when I spoke to him at his Torquay home. He was as vigorous, as pungent and as witty as ever in his views.

He has changed the name of his new play, *The Night Is Whispering*, to *The Drums Of Father Ned*.[1]

It is a comedy. 'There is absolutely no tragedy in it,' he said; 'I hope it will make people laugh.'

The play is written to the background of *An Tostal*, which incidentally is one of the Irish activities of which the 78-year-old playwright highly approves. 'I am all for festivities and for any attempt to put Ireland on the map—the Wexford Festival is a right good idea too,' he told me.

Like all O'Casey's work, the play, although it promises to be richly comic, will have a serious undercurrent.

O'Casey is also 'jotting down words' as he puts it for a future book, but it has not taken shape yet. The play is taking up most of his time.

However, he finds time to look occasionally at television. He saw the TV productions of his own plays and didn't like them very much. He has refused permission to have two of his other plays televised.

His objection to television as a medium for drama is based on artistic rather than personal reasons. He explains that TV does not convey the spirit of the play. And, also, the play is often cut drastically in order to fit a given time limit.

* *Irish Press* (Dublin), 18 September, 1957, p. 6.
† Journalist and reporter.

1. Subtitled 'A Mickrocosm of Ireland'.

O'Casey Says*

DON ROSS

Ross: Isn't there something rather strange about an Irish revolutionary like you coming to rest in England?

O'Casey: Something strange?

Ross: Well, here you are, a person who fought against England for a number of years. You were a revolutionary . . .

O'Casey: Not against England.

Ross: Well, against English soldiers.

O'Casey: Against the English government. The English government that meant to rule, and that they didn't understand and didn't want. I've always been against colonialism. I'm against French imperialism.

Ross: Do you think that this play of yours, *The Shadow of a Gunman*, has got anything to say to us today about politics? Is there a contemporary meaning?

O'Casey: Well, so they tell me . . . they tell me that it's philosophy rather than politics. I don't think there are any politics in the play— that is current politics. But it's philosophy, it's general philosophy.

Ross: What's the philosophy of the play?

O'Casey: Well, I think the general philosophy of the play is the bewilderment and horror at one section of the community trying to murder and kill the other. Against war, against strife. My philosophy is—speaking directly now—that life, life ought to be a safe thing to live. It oughtn't to be dangerous to live life, ought it? I think that all our efforts should be concerned with making life safe, not making it dangerous. That's why I'm against the hydrogen and all these atomic bombs and against war. I think they're making life dangerous instead of making life safe. That's my philosophy, and I think that's the philosophy that's in *The Shadow of a Gunman*.

* Extracted from *New York Herald Tribune*, 16 November, 1958, Section 4, p. 1. A trans-Atlantic telephone conversation between reporter Don Ross and Sean O'Casey on the gala occasion of two of O'Casey's plays being staged the same month in New York—*The Shadow of a Gunman* at the Bijou Theatre, and *Cock-a-Doodle Dandy* at Carnegie Hall Playhouse, off Broadway.

Ross: Why didn't you come to the United States for this gala O'Casey year?

O'Casey: Well, I'm a few months from seventy-nine. I've had seventy-nine strenuous years, and it's taken quite a bit out of me. The soul remains hale, the spirit remains strong, but the flesh is a little weak, you know. And I don't think I'd be able to withstand the generosity of the American people (*he laughs*). Don't mind that, because I love the American people, but I must say that the generosity of the American people is dangerous.

Ross: When was the last time you were in New York, Mr O'Casey?

O'Casey: I can't exactly say the year . . . it was the year of 1934 or 1935.[1]

Ross: Did you like it?

O'Casey: Oh, of course I liked it. The only complaint I had to make was that I had to get out of it. . . .

Ross: You had to get out of it? It sounds as though the sheriff might have been after you.

O'Casey: Well, my time was up, you know, I couldn't stay forever. Which was a great pity. But I had a most enjoyable time. I learned a lot from the American people. I learned a lot from their behaviour; the way they spoke; the way they went about; their buildings.

Ross: I want to get back to *The Shadow of a Gunman* for a moment. I've heard it said that in your plays it's the women who turn out to be the courageous ones.

O'Casey: Women must be more courageous than the men. Courage doesn't consist in just firing a pistol and killing somebody, or taking the risk of another firing a pistol and killing you. I wouldn't call that courage at all, I'd call it stupidity.

Ross: What does a woman's courage consist in?

O'Casey: Fortitude—and patience—and understanding.

Ross: Is this true, then, that you think that women are more courageous than men?

O'Casey: In life, yes. They're much more near to the earth than men are. Men are more idealistic, stupidly idealistic. They're not as realistic as women. The woman has to be nearer the earth than the man.

Ross: You like women, then?

O'Casey: Oh, I like men, too, provided they're not bores. But after all, women are half the population of the world—they're very im-

1. 1934: for the New York production of *Within the Gates*.

portant. What on earth would we do without them? (*laughter*)—I couldn't live in a house if there wasn't a woman.

Ross: How is your wife, incidentally?

O'Casey: Splendid. (*pause*) I like a pretty woman better than an ugly one. You remember what Emerson said about women. A woman that had a charming figure was very attractive, a woman that had a pretty face was very attractive, but that a woman with a pretty figure was more attractive, and that a woman that had a very charming nature was the most attractive of all, but when you put those three things together they make a very beautiful God's creation, don't they?

Ross: Did Emerson talk about women? I didn't know he was interested.

O'Casey: Waldo Emerson was interested in everything. Rivers and mountains, and pots and pans, and great revolutions, and antiquities of Greece and Rome. He was interested in everything that life showed him.

*   *   *

Ross: As a writer who is interested in freedom for writers, do you have any comment to make on the fact that Boris Pasternak, the Russian . . .

O'Casey: I wouldn't have any comment on that over the telephone. . . . The only comment that I would make is this: that from what I know and from what I feel, I think it was a sad mistake to expel Pasternak.[2] But I believe myself that the donation of the Nobel Prize had a political basis . . . it was due to a political cause . . . it was given to him for a wrong reason . . . it wasn't given to him that he was a great poet, but for political reasons. For instance, what makes me very bitter about this sort of thing is that there's no comment when other writers in other countries are persecuted. There was no one persecuted like James Joyce . . . there wasn't a voice raised to help him. Why didn't James Joyce get the Nobel Prize? He was probably one of the greatest writers in centuries. Yet the persecution of the man was appalling.

Ross: Have you read Pasternak's book? [3]

2. O'Casey expressed similar views, in a letter, dater 7 November, 1958, to O. Prudkov, Deputy Foreign Editor, *Literary Gazette* (Moscow).

3. *Doctor Zhivago*; English translation published in London in 1958.

O'Casey: No, I haven't. I couldn't. I don't know Russian.

Ross: It's been published in English translation, you know.

O'Casey: But I don't trust the English translation. I've read translations of my own. It's not anything, not anything like the original. All the spice and vigour, and revolution and Rabelaisian comedy in the original, they're all gone from the translation. It's a sad thing, this. I don't see why there should be these disputes about literature. I don't think they're necessary. I've never yet met a group of people that would hold the same opinion about a work of literature. You can't expect it. I've been condemned thousands of times in my own country for what I've written. And I can't help it. I think every artist should have freedom. Wasn't it Shakespeare that compared the poet with the lunatic? Every poet and every first-class artist they called a lunatic. Bernard Shaw, and Euripides, and Aeschylus and Shakespeare and all these men were close to lunacy.

Ross: Close to it, eh?

O'Casey: Close to it in so far as the curious visions they saw; the tremendous amount of evidence that they could throw out in front of them. They could see as many extraordinary things as any lunatic . . . or any lover. The lover, the lunatic and the poet, they all see the same thing. 'More devils than vast hell can hold,' on the one hand, and the lover seeing 'Helen's beauty in the brow of Egypt'. I don't see why the artist shouldn't have the same liberty as the lover and the lunatic.

Ross: You're for freedom for the artist.

O'Casey: Of course I am. I always have been.

Ross: But here is a situation in the Soviet Union where they have forced Pasternak to reject the Nobel Prize. Is this freedom?

O'Casey: Well, of course, that's their business, not mine. I was banned recently in Dublin, myself. Only recently they wouldn't let a play of mine [4] go on in Dublin. So you see, I know what it is. I experienced it.

Ross: Which one of your plays do you think was the most successful? Which one do you like the best?

O'Casey: Which way? You mean financially? As a drama?

Ross: Which one in your opinion was the best play?

O'Casey: My favourite's not necessarily the right one. If you want to know my favourite play, it's *Cock-a-Doodle Dandy*. I think that's

4. *The Drums of Father Ned*—withdrawn from the Irish Drama Festival, 1958.

the most cockeyed, and it's a ball from start to finish. It's by far the best of all I've written. That's my opinion.

Ross: Look, I've always been curious as to why you call yourself The Green Crow.

O'Casey: Well, I have great admiration for the crow. I always have had admiration for that particular bird. It's supposed to be the most intelligent bird in existence—the crow. More intelligent than most birds. All birds, practically. It's more a matter of degree. Although I don't look on myself as more intelligent than any other human being, I'm quite convinced that I have my share. Green, of course, is the national colour for Ireland. And there was a notice— a criticism of a recording of mine on a gramophone record—said of my voice, 'very interesting and fascinating, but as raucous as the cry of a crow'. So I thought it would be a good thing to call a book of essays, 'the caw of the green crow'. And I have a raucous voice at that. It's getting old and hoarse.

Ross: Mr O'Casey, thank you.

O'Casey: Well I hope you're not bored. I'm quite satisfied.

Au Revoir to the Abbey Theatre*

BARRY FITZGERALD †

To preserve a record of the Abbey Theatre, Dublin, before it was pulled down for rebuilding [1] *(the new Abbey was opened in 1966), some of its former illustrious members—including Siobhan McKenna, Cyril Cusack, Eileen Crowe—visited it to make a film. The half-hour film documentary, entitled* Cradle of Genius: A Tribute to the Abbey Theatre, *was made in Dublin by Plough Productions Ltd (1959), directed by Paul Rotha, and produced by Tom Hayes and Jim O'Connor.*

* Excerpt from the above-mentioned film.
† Distinguished Abbey actor and Hollywood film star.

1. The theatre was badly damaged by fire in 1951.

Actor Barry Fitzgerald and Sean O'Casey were two of the Abbey's greatest names. Fitzgerald went to see O'Casey in Torquay, after nearly thirty years, in connection with the film. To celebrate the occasion they sang a duet.

The following is a transcript of their conversation.

O'Casey: It's a grand thing to see you again, Barry, after such a long, long absence.

Fitzgerald: A long absence it is. Do you remember, Sean, that first night of *The Plough and the Stars*?

O'Casey: I do well; when the surrounding quietness of the Abbey Theatre was turned into a roar and a rush, and Yeats came bounding out on to the stage to oppose the howling mob, with his eyes flashing and his bushy hair waving like a bush that wasn't burning, and his arms extending over the yelling, bellowing dastards that tried to down the play, and he shouted out at them: 'You have disgraced yourselves again!' And then the roaring became worse and they shouted out against O'Casey. He roared out at them—with all the venom and vehemence that was in the great man—he shouted out at them: 'This is O'Casey's *apotheosis*' (probably because he had some peculiar belief in the magic of the word). Er—I wonder if those that were listening to him, Barry, knew the meaning of the word 'apotheosis'? Did *you*?

Fitzgerald: I'm not answering that question!

O'Casey: Did you understand?

Fitzgerald: No, of course I didn't!

O'Casey: You didn't? Well, then, neither did I! I was wondering about it all the way home, and it was a very late hour when I left; I was wondering all the way home what, in the name of God, was the meaning of 'apotheosis', and what had happened to O'Casey that he had had such an honour conferred on him. It was only when I got home, and, quietly and secretly, you know, looked up the dictionary I discovered that—O'Casey was translated up into the gods!

Fitzgerald: For me, the whole thing happened with that first production of *Juno and the Paycock*.

O'Casey: Ah, yes! It happened to me, too, when I met, for the first time, a most remarkable man and a great artist on that night of the first production of *Juno*, when I listened and heard your voice singing behind the wings—you know (*sings, in crusty voice, imitating 'Captain' Boyle's sonorous, self-honouring tones*):

'Sweet Spirit, hear me prayer! Hear . . .
   oh . . . hear . . . me prayer . . . hear, oh, hear . . .
   Oh, he . . . ar . . . oh, he . . . ar . . . me . . . pray . . . er!'

and you, Barry, who was going to be giving a glorious performance
that would add lustre not, maybe, to a great play but a funny one.
Sinclair [2] and the rest of them—and the ones that took part with you
in *Juno and the Paycock*—were good—and some of them splendid
—but, you, Barry, had that peculiar poetical touch in you that was
denied to so many—Sally Allgood had it, too, and Molly O'Neill [3]—
three great artists—and I have often since cursed the theatre that
drove such an artist as you were to seek a living in another medium;
for you, Barry, in my opinion (and it's no little opinion, either!)
you, Barry, were the greatest comedian that ever trod the English
stage.

Fitzgerald: Thank you very much, Sean.

O'Casey: And, now, Barry, we've talked a lot and I think it's
nearly time we took a little rest, and had a little rest with a drink;
but before we do that I'm going to give a little tinkle to that song
that you used to sing in the centre of the first act of the play:
(Sings):
'When the robins nest agen,
(Barry Fitzgerald joins in):

O'Casey
Fitzgerald } 'And the flowers are in bloom,
         When the Springtime's sunny smile seems to banish
               all sorrow an' gloom;
         Then me bonny blue-ey'd lad, if me heart be true
               till then—
         He's promised he'll come back to me,
         When the robins nest agen!'

2. Arthur Sinclair (1883–1951), who acted in the London productions of
O'Casey's early plays. He established himself as an Irish comedian.
3. Younger sister of Sara Allgood, who was married to Arthur Sinclair.

An Evening with
Sean O'Casey[*]

SAROS COWASJEE [†]

'Keep straight on till you come to the second traffic light, then turn right,' said a stiff-necked policeman without giving me a look. Was he a man or a slot machine? English, typically English. Had nothing better to point to than traffic lights. Ask a Dublin policeman to show you the way. 'Walk on, me frien', till ye come to Ryan's pub. Turn left if ye like, but if ye don't, walk on till ye come to Lawler's; then turn left and left again and there ye are.' You may never arrive, there's the rub, for there are too many temptations on the way. But what idle thoughts on such a day! Here I was on my way to see the greatest living Irishman—a man whom G. B. Shaw called a 'Titan', a dramatist whose plays London's leading dramatic critics described as 'blazing masterpieces, the greatest plays which have appeared in the English theatre since the days of the Elizabethans'. Would such a man see me? Was I really out to meet him? What if he turned round and said to his wife, in the words of Fluther Good, 'Be God, to think of a cur like that comin' to talk to a man like me!'

My confidence began to sag. I was not prepared to risk a step on Trumlands Road [1] before I had made certain where I stood. I pulled out his letter and read the first two sentences again : 'I should be very glad to have a chat with an "Indian Chap". We should be honoured in having one of your great people for a while in our home.'

It reassured me, though I could see that he had never met an Indian before. Good for him—just as well for me—he would see one soon. I rang the door-bell a little after four.

---

* *Illustrated Weekly of India* (Bombay), 17 May, 1959, p. 43. Also in *Irish Times* (Dublin), 25 July, 1959, p. 8.

† Author of *Sean O'Casey: The Man Behind the Plays* (Edinburgh and London : Oliver and Boyd, 1963; New York : St Martin's Press, 1964), and *O'Casey*, in the 'Writers and Critics' series (Edinburgh and London : Oliver and Boyd, 1966; New York : Barnes and Noble, 1967); together with several articles and reviews of books on the playwright. He teaches English at the University of Saskatchewan, Regina (Canada).

1. O'Casey's Torquay address.

Mrs O'Casey answered the bell. 'Come right in,' she said, leading me into a lovely drawing-room. 'Sean will be here soon.'

I settled down in the corner of a deep settee. The first thing that caught my eye was the famous portrait of O'Casey, by his friend Augustus John, engrossed in his own deep thoughts, lost to the world, lost even to the seductive charm of Paul Gauguin's *Ta Matete* hanging on the opposite wall.

O'Casey entered, took me by the hand and led me to the sofa. I kept staring at him. Could this frail little man, modestly dressed, a black Tashkent cap, embroidered in white—a size too big for him —on his head, and gold-rimmed spectacles with thick lenses be the O'Casey that I had imagined to myself? Could this old man of 79 be the same Johnny Casside I had read of? A young collarless labourer given to fierce resentment against all that was mean and sordid, a mad visionary dedicating himself to every progressive move-ment that held a gleam of hope for suffering humanity; a poor, self-educated young Protestant, who starved himself so as to save six-pences to buy himself books; a man who fought against every obstacle that came in his path with the determination to survive and become a great dramatist?

*   *   *

My doubts were brushed aside as he made me talk about the place I had come from and what I was doing. But I had not come 250 miles to talk about myself. Soon I was shooting questions at him about his plays. But he was not interested in them. 'What are they but a handful of dust,' he said. 'They are not worth anything.' I could not tell him that I had so delighted in his plays that I had often laughed aloud on the road when I thought of his comic creations— Joxer, Captain Boyle and Fluther Good, and only lately had I learnt to control myself for fear of being mistaken for a lunatic.

Seeing that he was not anxious to talk about his plays, I turned the conversation to Dublin.

'When will Dublin have permission to perform your plays?'

'Not till it produces those plays that were turned down by the Tostal Committee.' It was sad. In O'Casey's plays it is the innocent and the weak who suffer most in any war or revolution. In this feud between O'Casey and the Tostal Committee the victims again are the innocent—the innocent playgoers who revel in his plays.

'Do you still love Dublin?'

'Why, yes. I love the whole of Ireland. I don't differentiate between the North and the South '

There was an uneasy silence. I scratched my head for another question. God! Was that all I had to ask about Dublin? But O'Casey had a question this time. He leaned forward and with mischief in his eyes said to me:

'Tell me, you're not Irish?'

'No, yes—I am not Irish,' I said.

'You seem very interested in Ireland.'

'The Irish have a lust for life, and that draws me.' He leaned back on the sofa and sadly shook his head. 'That Ireland is gone,' he said. 'That Ireland is gone.' I stared at him. I could see his mind swim back to the agitated Dublin of his youth, and himself in front of every fray that promised a hope for his country's freedom.

O'Casey shook himself out of his reverie. 'Tell me something about India—about Nehru. I have great admiration for Nehru.'

'So have I but ... but will Dublin ...'

'Oh, talk to me about India. Who is the next man after Nehru?'

'I don't know. Nehru doesn't know either!' I replied.

'I never met Nehru, but Shaw did. But I saw Mahatma Gandhi and even heard him speak ... a great man, a saint, a great saint. Mind you. Gandhi was a pacifist while I am not. I believe in fighting for my rights. I heard Gandhi once, back in London. There was a meeting, and Gandhi stood on a low platform dressed in his loin-cloth; hand-woven, what do you call it? *Khaddar* ... *khaddar*, I get it now. After he had done his bit of speaking, a fellow, stretched on a seat in the front row, bawled at Gandhi, "Now will you tell me what is a Mahatma?" Gandhi looked at him, smiled, and said slowly and deliberately, "A Mahatma, sir, is a most insignificant person." '

I liked the way O'Casey narrated the incident in his soft, nasal voice. And as he enjoyed it as much as I did, I made him repeat the whole thing again at which I am sure he was delighted!

From India we drifted to China and Russia. He did not think that the recent happenings in China and Tibet meant much. Nor did he feel that India was in any way involved in this trouble. 'Communism is out to abolish poverty,' he said. 'We must do away with it. I hate the poor, for nothing can be done to help them. We must do away with the poor by abolishing poverty.'

He talked of Communism and what it meant to the world. 'Communists have always hated war; so do all sane men. I never lost my

Communism. It merely changed by growing deeper and more certain within me.'

'If you were always a Communist, how is it that you did not glorify them in your earlier plays as you have done in *The Star Turns Red*?' I asked.

O'Casey gave a significant reply, though one may disagree with it. 'Communists,' he said, 'have glorified themselves more effectively in the world than they have in plays or novels. Besides there is no Communistic dogma in *The Star Turns Red*. It is, as Shaw saw,[2] the spirit and prophecy of the Authorized Version of the English Bible.'

He talked affectionately of America. He said that 90 per cent of his income came from the United States. 'They have a lot of money. Must say that they have done a lot of good, too. But they could do more—more with the amount of money they have. Recently I was offered $2,500 for an article of 2,000 words. God! I needed the money, but I didn't like the paper. I refused.'

'But why?' I exclaimed.

'Why? Why should they pay an old man like me that sum for a short article? Why not give a chance to a young and struggling writer?'

That is Sean O'Casey's Communism—a crazy love and concern for the poor and neglected. His communism is not a political dogma, it owes nothing to Russia. 'Russia is not Communist,' he told me. 'It will take another 60 years before it goes Communist. Your India may take as much as 150 years.'

*   *   *

At 7.30 his wife suggested that Mr O'Casey should have a little rest, and that in the meantime I should have a meal with her in town. Soon we were seated in a cosy café overlooking the beach. I found Mrs O'Casey intelligent, kind, and very charming. She talked about her recent visit to New York,[3] of her husband's work and how he is easily tired, of the lack of enterprising producers and honest theatre critics. All this, punctuated frequently by a loud, gay laugh—a laugh that must remind O'Casey of the gay laugh of his mother.

*   *   *

2. Letter to O'Casey, dated 22 April, 1940; quoted in *Sean*, p. 177.
3. On the occasion of the American première of *Cock-a-Doodle Dandy*.

When we returned at 9.30 I suggested that I leave as Mr O'Casey must be tired.

'Sit down, man,' said O'Casey. 'I am not tired.'

He was now more willing to talk about things he had earlier brushed aside. Here are some of his assertions:

'I like all my plays. *Cock-a-Doodle Dandy* is my favourite, though *The Plough and the Stars* is my best play.

'I enjoy thinking and planning out my plays but hate writing.

'I am not anti-Catholic. I only attack some of its practices which I think to be wrong.

'All my characters in all my plays are taken from real life. I knew "Captain" Boyle very well—a splendid drunkard, but a rotten husband.

Yeats was the greatest poet of our age. A little vain and proud at times, but he was justified in being so.

'The Abbey Theatre collapsed with the death of Yeats.

'Nietzsche is out of date: Schopenhauer is too pessimistic for me.'

He also had some advice for me:

'Don't waste your time in the British Museum or any other library. There are many better things that you can do.[4]

'Forget your work. What difference will it make whether you succeed or fail? The more important thing in life is to live.'

At 11.30 I made to go. 'There is no need for you to hurry. Stay on as long as you want to,' he said.

But I was determined to go, though I would have loved to stay on longer. I had not the heart to take advantage of O'Casey's infinite goodness. He sent for a taxi and insisted on paying for it. All the way back I thought of this man—the man who was greater than his works.

Back in my hotel room, I opened my copy of *I Knock at the Door* that I had asked him to autograph. This is what he had written:

Inscribed to my friend, Saros Cowasjee, by
Sean O'Casey.
Hurrah for India!
and
for Ireland too!
Devon, 1959[5]

4. At this time the author was working for his PhD on O'Casey at the University of Leeds.

5. O'Casey, on reading this interview, wrote to Cowasjee in his letter dated 5 July, 1959: 'I liked the *Illustrated India* [sic] very much; very colorful and

gay-looking; tho' I don't think it so good as the earlier *India* published in the Thirties, which was much more Socialistic. . . . Your article was good, but too, too kind. I am not half as good as you evidently think. I have yet many, many things to learn.' (Unpublished letter in Cowasjee's possession.)

The Exile*

W. J. WEATHERBY †

Weatherby: You were once quoted as saying you were an exile from everything.

O'Casey: I never accept anything that has not my name to it because many things have been said about me that are not true. I have never been exiled from life and that is the only thing that matters. I'll be exiled enough when I go off at the end from all the things I love and participate in. Most of the modern writers are so god-damn gloomy. They reject life in every concept, yet they cling to it if they get a cold or a fever and rush to the doctor and appeal to him to set them on the road again. You'd think they would welcome the way to the tomb, but they don't. I want to live as long as I'm active and can more or less look after myself and not be a burden or a nuisance to myself. I can't understand how the hell any young man is despairing in life.

Weatherby: What do you think about our ways of preparing people for life?

O'Casey: I'm against any prison system of education in high school, secondary school, or university. Packing with facts to the point of suffocation is an extraordinary way of drawing out a human mind. But I'm no authority on education. Lots of people make the mistake of thinking when I say something I mean to be positive about it. I just have an opinion like anyone else. Oxford and Cambridge, the king and queen of English universities, have a monopoly of influence and fame they ought not to have. The best of the education that comes out of them is due to the opportunities offered for students to come together and hold discussions.

* Extracted from 'Figure in the Shadows' [interview at O'Casey's home in Torquay], *Manchester Guardian*, 10 September, 1959, p. 6.
† English author, journalist and novelist.

Weatherby: Do you believe in communism, in politics generally, that power corrupts. . . .

O'Casey: Oh, you Liberals are all alike. You always trot out that saying. . . .

Weatherby: I'm nearer an anarchist than that. . . .

O'Casey: Anarchism is a high philosophical state. Remember, we must do our best with what we have. We can't just say 'No' to life. It is regrettably true that every great change has brought upset and suffering, whether it's the Industrial Revolution or communism. Soviet communism as far as I know is a Russian system. It is peculiar to the Russian people. English communism when it comes, as it will eventually, will not be the same at all. An Englishman can't be a Russian any more that you can make an Irishman an Englishman. I saw a Russian come over here to teach drama—a nephew of Chekhov, Michel Chekhov. He taught the Russian Stanislavsky way of acting. But it didn't suit the English. They couldn't do it. They looked laughable when they appeared on the stage. The English must act his own way, so must the Irish, and the Scot is different from both. The only similarity is that they all speak the same language—a great advantage.

Weatherby: Is the English style no good for your plays?

O'Casey: I remember one actress. She was no damn good. So I think it was the director who said Beatrix Lehmann could do it. She didn't look as though she could. But by God she gave a wonderful performance. You can never decide with artists what they can do. An artist can almost do anything—if he's got genius of course. But the English as a whole find it difficult to get the Irish lilt and they put on an accent which is terrible. There are 32 accents in Ireland. Every county has got one. Look how the English way of speech varies. (*He did some imitations.*) The West here is a very homely and hospitable part, very unspoilt. They're well away from London. The Home Counties are suffocated by London manners. I never met the English people until I penetrated into the country. When you get away from London the English people are truly English. They live their English way and are very, very charming. But in London, they get spoilt, I think.

Weatherby: How long ago is it since a play of yours was produced in London?

O'Casey: I don't know. Some time during the war, was it? About fifteen years.

Weatherby: Why do you think your plays have been so neglected?

O'Casey (puzzled): I don't know. Perhaps, as the man said, it is because of my politics. Or is it that I write bad plays?

Mrs O'Casey: Perhaps they are a bit too good.

O'Casey: My plays I hope always have a good deal of humour in them.

Mrs O'Casey: Perhaps what is fashionable to-day is something a little vague, like Eliot's *The Cocktail Party.*

O'Casey: Eliot's integrity is undoubted. I always had a great respect for him. I reprobated the Soviet Union for attacking Eliot because he's a very honest man. He admits to being an old Tory and a churchman. No one should mind an honest enemy. What you have to be afraid of is a dishonest friend.

Weatherby: What were you aiming at when you changed from the realistic style of *Juno*?

O'Casey: I had no aim except to try to write a good play. Nobody lives without a touch of fantasy.[1] I can't stand these little trivial realistic things. The change in my style came spontaneously. I didn't want to restrict the range of the theatre. Neither did Shakespeare. It's not all O'Casey. Shakespeare is full of fantasy, symbolism, song and dance. You would think it's something new. Shakespeare of course is allowed to do it because he is in the English canon. A cult began for realism and it lasted for a while and reached its peak. Nobody could excel the realism of O'Neill.

Weatherby: When O'Neill died, *Time* magazine said only Shaw and you outranked him among twentieth-century dramatists.

O'Casey: That was kind of them. But not *Time* the magazine but time itself is the only critic which can say whether a man is great or not great. Time discards a hell of a lot of things.

Weatherby: Do you speak your dialogue aloud as you write?

O'Casey: I think in dialogue. But I don't like talking about my work at all. I can't stand the early stuff like *Juno* and *The Plough* as a matter of fact. Realism comes too easy in a way. I think I can create a character and put dialogue into his mouth but I'm not satisfied to do only that.

Mrs O'Casey: It's a pity Sean hasn't had a theatre or a group in which to try out his plays before they were presented to the public.

O'Casey: I would have liked that. I remember seeing a play of mine [2] acted in the United States and thinking some part of it was

1. *Blasts and Benedictions*, pp. 82–4.   2. *Within the Gates.*

underwritten. Watching the acting, I discovered I had taken all the leading characters off the stage at the same time. It was not unbearably dull but it was comparatively dull. I rewrote the whole play.[3] If I had had somewhere to run it through, I would have seen that so much sooner. Every town should have a municipal theatre with equal vision from every seat in the house.

Weatherby: Do you miss your connections with the Abbey Theatre?

O'Casey (sternly): I don't think so. I miss the few hundreds a year I had. But I'm told they can't act now. Anyway I've banned my plays in Ireland since the trouble last year over *Drums of Father Ned.* I'm not going to submit any of my plays with the chance of an archbishop speaking against them. Theatre people in Dublin get just a bit jittery when that happens.

*   *   *

Mr O'Casey broke off to search for his tobacco and also showed me his colourful skull-cap, part of his great collection of head-gear.[4] He then launched into a wonderful story about the old Dublin militia, complete with imitations of the principal characters. Through the smoke and laughter, he confided: 'You know, if I had my time over again I would not take up writing. It is too precarious a living. I would take up something like engineering.' But with his talent, had he a choice? He replied with feeling: 'I didn't have the choice of being an engineer when I was a boy.'

3. The text of the first edition, 1933, differs considerably from that of the stage version, printed in *Collected Plays*, volume 2, 1949.
4. A symbol, in later years, of the gay, free and intrepid life and outlook he always so vigorously defended.

O'Casey Did Not Celebrate 80th Birthday*

Sean O'Casey, the Irish playwright, who was 80 on 30 March, 1960, did not celebrate the occasion. 'Why should I?—It is just the same as any other day,' he said at his Torquay home. He spent most of the day writing.

'I never have or never will take any interest in birthdays,' he told me. 'What good will birthdays do anybody? I have no time for this good-will Christian charity business on one day of the year only—it should exist all the year around.'

*   *   *

Mr O'Casey said that he would never return to live in Ireland. 'I couldn't stick it,' he declared. 'Neither could Shaw. I am not anti-Irish—I am very much for the people of Ireland. It is the establishment that I am against.'

Ireland had a future, he declared, but it was with her young people.[1] That was why it depressed him so much to see the young flocking out of the country. 'They will keep on going,' he asserted, 'so long as they are held down as they are. There won't be any future for the young in Ireland until we create a present for them.'

*   *   *

Mr O'Casey said that there was no Irish theatre because people in Ireland were too much afraid of offending. This was due to the fact that they had no conception of the Catholic faith. The faith embraced the whole company of the faithful, laymen as well as clergy. It was not confined to bishops. 'The Pope is said to have the key to Heaven,' he added, 'but it seems to me that every Irish bishop has a master key.'

Mr O'Casey declared that one of the great tragedies of Irish emigra-

---

* *Irish Times* (Dublin), 31 March, 1960, p. 9.

1. The theme of his play, *The Drums of Father Ned*.

tion was that it was the young and vigorous who were leaving. There was a danger that eventually Ireland would become almost depopulated in the end.[2] The Government should consider the problem.

2. *The Vanishing Irish*, ed. J. A. O'Brien (London, 1954).

Drumming with Father Ned*

DAVID PHETHEAN †

'I'm a Communist!' said Sean O'Casey. 'Did ye know that?'

'Yes,' I said, a trifle non-plussed. 'I did.'

'Well, of course, I know that I'm a hero over in Russia, because they never stop tellin' me, but I don't go out of my way to say particularly nice things about them.'

I asked him if he'd been over there recently.

'No, I've never been to Russia,' he said. 'They keep askin' me to go, and what with hairy-o-planes, I could be there for lunch!'

'Why don't you go?' I asked.

'I'm too old now,' he said. 'They'd over-wellum me! I'd ev-ah-porate!' He laughed loudly. 'No,' he said finally. 'It's a young man's country.'

'Would you describe the Russian Government as "Communist"?' I asked.

'No,' he said firmly. 'It's not. They're trying hard, of course. Perhaps in another hundred and fifty years or so. But *you* should go and work there. It's the only place for a young man to work if you're in the teatre. (He made it sound like 'teerter'.) You can't work here. There's no teatre left in this country now. Over there the government pours money into the teatre because the people *want* it, and they think the people should have it! Did you know that'n Russia is the only country in the world where actors are not allowed to play at bein' soldiers? Even in wartime? Did ye know that?! . . .

* This interview was never published, although reference is made to it by Eileen O'Casey in her book, *Sean*, p. 272. It is here reproduced by kind permission of the interviewer.

† Actor and theatre director. At present with Bristol Old Vic Company. Directed the British première of *The Drums of Father Ned* at the Queen's Theatre, Hornchurch (Essex), in November 1960.

Mind you, they have to take their teatre to the trenches. But can you imagine anything like that happenin' in this country?'

I agreed that our attitude was philistine by comparison, but that I thought we were managing to break it down slowly. . . .

'How?' he challenged.

'Well (I said) the war achieved one important advance. It set the precedent of Government patronage of the Arts in this country.'

'And how has that helped?' he asked.

'The Arts Council (I said) assists theatres, like Hornchurch, financially. . . .'

He interrupted sharply and derisively.

'Arts Council! What can they do? They're only subsidising empty seats! What's the use in that? It's bottoms you want on seats—not pound notes! How can you act a play to empty seats? What's the point in that? Nobody's *interested* in the teatre in this country. They're only interested in making money. All the working man wants is his foot-ball pools and his motor-car. He doesn't want the teatre. He never has. It's the same now as when I wrote about it in the twenties! . . . Have you read my book *The Flying Wasp*?'

I regretted the omission.

'It was published in 1937 or thereabouts. But they didn't want to poblish it!' He smiled with pleasure at the recollection. 'They tried to stop it!'

I asked him why.

'Well I'll tell you. . . . It was a vithriolic attack on the English teatre in general—and on Noël Coward in particular. I sent the manuscript to Misther Mack-Millun.' He shot me a quick glance. 'You've heard of *him*, I suppose? He's your Prime Minister ye know.' (His tone implied that, though I might be ignorant of his books, he hoped that my general knowledge was sound.) I nodded and smiled. 'Well, he's also my poblisher. I sent him the manuscript, and I didn't hear anything more for quite a long while. So . . . I wrote Mack-Millun a letter askin' him if he'd lost it! Of course, I *knew* what was happenin' . . . (he chuckled happily). He was frightened of it! I'd sent him a lomp of dynamite! He couldn't make up his mind which would cause him more throuble—rejectin' it or poblishin' it! If he rejected it, he knew I'd send it to a rival poblisher, and if he poblished it, he knew that the whole of London's teatrical hierarchy would come down on him for a thraitor! Well I got a letter back from him askin' me if I really wanted to poblish it! So I replied that "Of course I wanted to poblish it! Why d' ye think I wrote it?!" and I asked him "what was the matter with it?" In reply, he asked me if I wouldn't mind goin' to see him at his office. He started by remindin' me that I earned my bread and butter from the teatre, and I said that I hadn't come to his office to be reminded of that, and was he offerin' me the reminder as a reason for my not tellin' the truth? He replied by sayin' that he thought the book was libellous, and I said:

' "Not at all. How can the truth be libellous?"

' "The 'truth' is a matter of o-pinion," he says.

' "How?" I said. "My o-pinion is that the truth is the truth, and I leave my reader to be my judge. What's *your* o-pinion?"

'Well, he tried to wriggle out of it by sayin' . . .

' "It's a little like brawlin' in church!" So I looked at him an' I said:

' "Misther Mack-Millun, are you a Christian . . . ?"

' "Yes," says he, "I am."

'I said, "I mean: Do you believe in Jesus Christ . . . ?"

'Well, he thought for a moment, and then he said:

' "Yes. I do." So I said:

' "And what was *He* doin' but brawlin' in the Temple?!"

'Mack-Millun had no answer to that, so I won! The book was published and it caused a stinkin' row, which was what I had hoped for it!'

I asked him if he was writing anything at the moment.

'No,' he replied, 'I can't see to write well. I get tired easily and then I can't concentrate. I don't write plays any more.'

'How about *Father Ned*, then?' I asked.

'I just wrote it for fun,' he replied. 'And then I was asked by Brendan Smith,[1] the Director of the Doblin International Teatre Festival, if I would give them a play to perform for old time's sake, as part of the annual Tostal celebrations. It was to be a jolly occasion, so I gave them a jolly play. But the Archbishop of Doblin banned it because he said it was blasphemous, and so it was never performed.'[2]

*   *   *

1. The text of the correspondence between O'Casey and Brendan Smith is included in *A Paler Shade of Green*, ed. Des Hickey and Gus Smith (London, 1972), pp. 134–51.

2. It was later performed in Dublin, at the Olympia Theatre, 6 June, 1966.

The Drums of Father Ned is a crackerbarrel of O'Casey 'o-pinions'. It is his happiest play—or rather, as one critic put it, a 'liberation', his aim being, simply, 'to cry life'. A group of villagers are preparing to celebrate the Tostal, the Irish Folk Festival. All is gaiety, laughter, singing and dancing. The parish priest—an outraged, umbrella-waving pillar of the Established Church—tries desperately to restrain the rumbustious spirits of his flock while they, in turn, excuse themselves by crying: 'It's all Father Ned's work!' . . . Father Ned, whom the bewildered parish priest angrily seeks but can never find; for Father Ned is a spirit—part playboy, part radical Catholic priest— O'Casey's greater spirit of humanity, and his tribute to those few friends in the priesthood, to whom he dedicates the play and of whom he says: '*The Memory be Green*'; all of whom 'broke the rules' in order to reach the suffering humanity in their care. '*Each in his time,*' writes O'Casey, '*was a Drummer for Father Ned, and the echoes of their drumming sound in Ireland still!*'

Our discussion of the play was constantly deflected by some chance word or remark, which would start a chain-reaction of reminiscence or comment. The word 'yellow' for example, which occurs in one of his stage directions. There is a prologue to the play, which O'Casey calls, characteristically, '*The Prerumble*', in which a group of 'Black and Tans' accost a couple of Republicans engaged in a private argument. The 'Black and Tans' were those hated British police auxiliaries at the time of the 'throubles', who were recruited from renegade Irishmen, though as O'Casey pointed out . . . :

'They were renegade only because they had mouths to feed, and they were desperate for money for food and drink.' And he went on . . . 'The country was starvin' ye know, at the time! People were litherally dyin' where they dropped in the sthreet! There wasn't enough of *anythin*'. And it was the same with clothin'. The British recruited these renegades—if they hadn't been shot by their own countrymen first—and then found that there weren't enough po-lice uniforms to put them into. So they dressed them in Irish Constabulary jackets—which aren't "black" as it happens, they're dark green, but they look black from a distance—and British Army trousers or vicey versah.'

'I realise that,' I replied, 'but your stage direction indicates that they should wear "black jackets and yellow trousers". When you write "yellow", do you mean "khaki"?'

'No,' he snapped, 'I mean "yeller"!' and, pushing his spectacles once more on to his forehead, he glanced swiftly about the room, muttering 'yeller ... yeller ...'.

'Here!' he cried, 'give me that cushion.'

He indicated one lying on his sofa, and when I brought it to him, he held it to his face, almost touching the end of his nose.

'No,' he muttered in irritation, '*That's* not yeller. I mean *yeller*! Why do you want kar-*kee*!?'

'Only (I said) for the sake of realism. ...'

'What do you want with "realism"!?' he cried. 'The teatre isn't the place for *that*! You can see more than enough "realism" any time you walk along the pavements! My mother had thirteen children, of whom eight died in childhood. *That's* realism! There was so little money I had a daily dose of "realism" in my belly. It was comin' up through the soles of my bare feet! ... Realism! ... huh! ... Did you know that I started writing when I was sixteen and I was over forty before I had any work poblished? What d'ye think I did in the meantime!?'

'I can imagine,' I said quietly, as he paused for breath.

'I *had* to earn money or the family would go without their one proper meal a day. ... ! No. (His voice mellowed.) The teatre is a place of magic. It should be full of colour and excitement and gaiety. That's what it's *there* for! To bring colour into people's lives! ... You know, I've never forgotten one of my first visits to the Abbey Theatre in Doblin. In Lady Gregory's time. You'll have heard of her, I suppose... ?'

'Yes indeed,' I replied.

'*She* was the genius behind the Abbey, you know. A lot of people think it was Yeats, but it wasn't. Mind you, he was useful to the Theatre. He gave it prestige. And he liked the limelight. He got a lot of the kudos for standin' by me on the platform when my play *The Plough and the Stars* was bein' howled down by the mob. But Lady Gregory was the *real* genius. She was a marvellous woman ... selfless, single-minded. ... She came of an old, aristocratic, land-ownin' family, and she really cared for Ireland and Irish literature and the Gaelic tongue. It was she who found and inspired and encouraged the writers, and told them what to write, and how to write it. It was she made the Abbey what it was ... well ... what was I sayin'? ... oh yes ... Colour! ... I remember this particular scene because it was so vivid: There was just this great big aquamarine sky, fillin' the whole of the back of the stage, and all that was placed in front of it was a large red triangular sail of a boat! It was so simple an effect, and so beautiful, that I've never forgotten it. It was sublime!'

He made this simple image so striking, and, by inference, so revealing of his aims for *Father Ned*, that I promised him all the colour I could give it. Once the play was running, I had some colour photographs taken and these I sent to him as a keepsake.

'Tell me about *your* teatre,' he said.

I told him briefly how it had been built as a cinema in the thirties, was a warehouse during the war, and how the local council had converted it themselves into a fully-equipped theatre in the early fifties, thereby becoming the first truly 'civic' theatre in the country.

'Fully-equipped?' he said. 'How? Can you fly scenery? How big is the stage?'

I gave him the dimensions.

'Not very big,' he replied. 'My plays need space. And they need a lot of equipment. Are there good sight-lines? How many does it seat?'

'Just under 400,' I replied.

'That's very little,' he said. 'It must have been one o' them bee-jew cinemas, with straight walls. Can you put Shakespeare on your stage?'

I replied that we could and did.

'I don't see how you can make it pay. Shakespeare's expensive!'

I reminded him that we had to lean heavily on an Arts Council Grant, and apropos, I took the opportunity of asking him what he would expect in the way of royalty. He didn't answer immediately.

'How much do you charge for your seats?' he asked.

'Prices range (I said) from six shillings down to three shillings.'

He paused for a moment.

'Do they allow standin' in the aisles?'

'I'm afraid the fire authorities would object to that,' I said.

'They allowed standin' in the aisles at the Abbey—but only for *my* plays, mind!' He chuckled. 'They were too successful! There'd have been a riot if they hadn't! Don't worry about royalties. I won't break your bank!'

He asked me about the company.

'I am recruiting them at this moment,' I said, adding that I would enlarge the regular group to include a number of good Irish actors when I started on *Father Ned*.

'Why?' he snapped.

'English actors,' I said, 'would probably have difficulty with the rhythms and accent. . . .'

'Never mind the hac-cent,' he broke in. 'All you want are good actors! The only hactin' I ever attempted was with an English group of ama-*turs*. I was the only foreigner amongst them, but nobody minded the way *I* spoke!'

'Were you a success?' I asked.

'I was dreadful! Ap-PALL-in'! I wasn't asked again!'

A moment later Mrs O'Casey came in with the tea, and we talked about their family. About Shivaun at Bristol, and about Breon, her brother, who is a sculptor, and was working down in Cornwall.

'He enjoys it,' O'Casey said. 'But I don't suppose he'll make any money at it!'

*   *   *

I left soon after tea, with the great man's permission to produce his play, and his good wishes for its success. I only had two more communications from him, and the first concerned the Censor, whose permission had to be obtained before the play could be performed. I have mentioned the Black and Tans in the 'Prerumble'. Their leader tries to patch up the quarrel between the two Republicans with the phrase: *'Shake hands, you blighted buggers!'* This expletive is on the Censor's black list (though my Oxford Dictionary gives it a perfectly respectable pedigree, which reads: From the French 'bougre', derived from the Latin 'Bulgarus', an 11th-century heretic from Bulgaria, supposed capable of any crime). I wrote asking O'Casey for an alternative, and he sent back *'Bullynoors'*, adding the laconic note: *'You are quite safe with this one. The Lord Chamberlain won't know whether it's dirty or daycent!'*

The second and last communication came after the production had ended. It had had a *'succès d'estime'*, but I have to admit that Hornchurch was puzzled by it. Shivaun came to see it and duly reported back to her father, taking my working copy with her. I had made some ruthless textual changes in order to clarify the general theme for an English audience. When I think back, I am astonished at my temerity. After reading the newspaper criticisms—and my working copy—O'Casey wrote back as follows:

'Dear Mr Phethean, I don't like your cuts, and, if I had been there, I wouldn't have allowed most of them. I don't write plays which are easy, nor do I write parts for actors which they can play "standing on their heads". However, I make allowance for the fact that you only had a fortnight for rehearsals when four weeks would hardly have been sufficient. I also make allowance for the lack of technical equipment in your theatre, which I know is small. In spite of this, it is obvious that you have given a vigorous account of the play, which, as Shivaun has told us, was full of life and colour, for which I am grateful, and which I felt, when I met you, you would be able to accomplish, otherwise I would not have allowed you to do it. It is also obvious from the newspaper comments that they did not understand what I was about, except, perhaps, the *New Statesman*,[3] which came somewhere near it. Please accept my deep and sincere gratitude for all that you have done for the play, and all the hard work which you and the Company have put into it.

Sincerely, Sean O'Casey.'

I felt suitably chastened and I reflected soberly. The late George Devine used to say that when a playwright brings a new play into the theatre, he is carrying a bucket of blood, and he must expect some of it to be spilt! What would he have said, I wondered, to spilling the blood of Ireland's Shakespeare? And yet, having committed this heinous crime, I received my working copy back, autographed and inscribed in the author's own hand: '*With my thanks for a good production. Sean O'Casey.*'

3. H. A. L. Craig's review, 'Red Roses for O'Casey', 19 November, 1960, p. 782.

O'Casey Plays Not for TV*

AIDAN HENNIGAN †

The ban which Sean O'Casey has put on the professional production of his plays in Ireland may be extended to their presentation on Irish television.

* *Irish Press* (Dublin), 9 May, 1961, p. 3.
† London editor of the *Irish Press* (Dublin).

The playwright told me that he did not consider television a suitable medium for his plays. 'I do not want my plays hacked and cut. They simply would not be my plays any more,' he said.

Commenting on the future of Irish television, he said it should be good if properly run. He hoped that Gael Linn [1] would get a say in its management.

Of Brendan Behan he said: 'It's sad to see this man abusing himself like he is. If he does not mind his talent it will fade.'

Turning to the Nelson Pillar controversy, O'Casey suggested that a group of five literary figures—Yeats, Lady Gregory, Joyce, Shaw and himself—should be erected on the Pillar instead of Nelson. However, he did not mind if other Irish figures were erected instead: 'Someone like Wolfe Tone [2] or Eoin MacNeill [3] would be much more suitable up there than Nelson.'

O'Casey added that he did not mean any disrespect to Nelson, as he regarded him as a great English admiral, but he felt that even Wellington—who had Dublin associations—would be more fitting.

1. Newest and most active of the Gaelic Societies (formed in 1953), exploiting the mass media and other techniques to pull Gaelic out of the doldrums.
2. Founder of the Society of United Irishmen (1791).
3. Vice President of the Gaelic League (1893).

The Cross and the Shamrock*

HUGH WEBSTER

Webster: Stirring up controversy has been a knack Sean O'Casey has always had. He has styled himself 'The Green Crow', and he says himself that he always has to speak and speak while he seeks and finds his food and so has had less meat than he might have had if only he'd kept his big beak shut.[1] An opinion to O'Casey is something you own and your conscience insists you share it with others.

O'Casey: For to have a thing is nothing if you've not a chance to

* A shortened transcript of the Canadian Broadcasting Corporation's discussion programme, 'Conscience and Sean O'Casey', in the 'Project 62' series, transmitted on 29 October, 1961. Commentary and production were by Hugh Webster.

1. *The Green Crow* (1956), Foreword, xiv.

show it, and to know a thing is nothing unless others know you know.

Webster: Listening to him one gets the impression that he loves nothing better than a conversation providing there's a chance of disagreement. He keeps dropping little phrases every now and then, which are almost challenges, to step out and fight.

O'Casey: I don't see why we should be murdering each other at all, whether even . . . whether even if we aren't Christians. It's only the Christians who start killing each other, as far as I know; the pagans or heathens are much more tolerant of each other than the Christians are. I don't say they war now for religion but they war for something else that's even worse because there may be some justification for fanatics believing their God is the right one and slaying other people because they don't want to accept that opinion. That's the kind of idealism that isn't as bad as warring for economic reasons. We're all part of the universe; we're all, if you can use the Christian saying, we're all God's children, though some of us won't speak to some of the others . . . well, the United States refusing to have anything to do with China; they won't speak to China. I don't know why. I suppose China's not Christian, is she? Doesn't matter whether she's Christian or not because the fact of a person not being Christian doesn't make God any less a father if the Christians believe in what they teach.

Webster: Always an eye open for the possible explosion, the opponent who will snatch up a challenge and will bring on the clash. Like many an Irishman, he wants a fight as well as a joke, a tear as well as a song, and this is the double edge one finds in his plays as they come roaring into the theatre, enticing the Irishmen to laugh, to cry, to sing, and to fight. . . . As a result of his ironic view of the Irish, their struggle for independence and their Church, O'Casey's plays and opinions have always met with something less than unanimous approval in Ireland, but throughout the world he is recognised as the greatest living playwright of the English-speaking theatre. . . . Having settled in England, he had three important plays behind him, *The Shadow of a Gunman*, *Juno and the Paycock*, and *The Plough and the Stars*—plays that have become known as O'Casey's great plays. But now he wanted something new—a new form to his writing. Fantasy and expressionism replaced the lovingly vulgar realities of the old masterpieces and immediately everyone demanded a return to the kind of play he used to write: the plays the same people had condemned not too long ago; and being O'Casey he made sure they did not get them. Writing according to his conscience he turned out his new plays, *The Silver Tassie*, *Red Roses for Me*, *Purple Dust*, *Cock-a-Doodle Dandy*, and in 1955 came *The Bishop's Bonfire*, a play that expressed fully an opinion which O'Casey held for a long time and which had earned him many enemies. O'Casey considers Ireland's chief fault is her overpowering chastity, imposed, he feels, by the Irish church. He sees a fading of her colour as the country turns away from life. His new play was in Dublin after a long absence and it was a play that took the church to task. It seemed like a gala occasion and O'Casey was only too happy to talk about it.

O'Casey: A play of mine hadn't been done in Dublin for years and a young producer and an actor, very fine actor, named Cyril Cusack, wrote to me and said—or intimated to me—that he'd heard I had written a play and would I send him the script. I'm very fond of this young fellow and his wife, I know the family well. I sent it to him and he said he'd love to do it and I said very well, go ahead but you've read the play and it may give you a great deal of trouble. I warned him against producing it because I liked him—I didn't want to cause him any pain or place him in any difficulty but he determined to go on and he produced . . . he rehearsed the play and it was to open on a certain night in one of the biggest theatres in Dublin, almost the biggest—the one where all the big professional plays are produced, the Gaiety Theatre. Well that night . . . it was an appalling event really . . . because it caused so much excitement. Now this is a fact, I'm not saying it because I'm just the author, it just happens to be a fact—it caused such an immense amount of excitement that everybody wanted to see it and consequently all around the theatre . . . all the roads around the theatre were blocked . . . the traffic around all the roads surrounding the theatre were blocked by the crowd. Traffic couldn't pass through them and of course the theatre couldn't accommodate one hundredth part of the people that wanted to get in and there were a number . . . oh, a number of the men I knew, and the sons of the men I knew from my younger days in the labour movement—they lighted bonfires in the streets of Dublin, near the theatre, as a kind of, well, tribute to one whom they liked so much for standing up for the working class in Ireland in the early days . . . and the attempt . . . the crowds were so great and so massive that the police couldn't possibly control them. There weren't any riots or any violence, all good humour, but the police couldn't keep a way opened for those who had booked seats, you see, to get in, and your own Commissioner, the Commissioner of Canada, although he'd booked a first class seat, couldn't get near the theatre and neither could Madam Pandit who was the Indian Ambassador to Ireland. She had a seat there but she had to wait another two nights before she could get in. Quite a number of what are called distinguished people hadn't a chance of getting in the theatre because of this immense interest that was taken in the play and of course it played to crowded houses the whole time it was presented and I'm very glad to say that the young man that ventured to accept and put it on, made a good deal of money out of it and that pleased me very much.

Webster: An Irishman can be forgiven for seeing this play as a plea for Ireland to turn away from what to O'Casey is the pale shadow of the church, to the riper colours of the world of men and women, but the English director of the London production of the play, Frank Dunlop, sees the theme as a more universal one.

Dunlop: O'Casey looks at both sides of every question and when he talks about religion there's a ridiculous figure and a sensible one, so he puts both sides of the question every time as a problem. He's not biased at all, and of course if you're very sensitive about the silly things in religion or the silly things in life, well, then, you'll think that he's criticising you and you'll start shouting things in the first performance. The play's not anti-clerical, it's just anti-everything that's silly in life, and pro-everything that's good in life. It's a very youthful play and very pro-anything that will open up life for people.

Webster: And, of course, O'Casey himself has something to say about the universality of the play and other related topics.

O'Casey: You can't write about universal problems because you don't know them, but you can unite the individual and the local problems into the universe and we're all members of the universe. Take *The Bishop's Bonfire,* for instance. It deals with a special period and a special event, but on the other hand it also deals with the great global problem that has gone on since man started to have definite religious opinions. The great war between State and Church —they've always been antagonistic. The one has always tried to conquer the other. The contest between church and state has gone on between every Christian country on the globe . . . in France . . .

and I suppose it's going on now in the United States. You had recently the Cardinal Archbishop of New York—his name is Cardinal Spellman—rebuking Mrs Roosevelt because she stood by the letter of the constitution refusing to give any state aid to schools under clerical jurisdiction, remember that? Well, that's an instance of the intolerance and impertinence of a cleric talking to a secular citizen. A person just as distinguished and much more intellectual than himself.

Webster: O'Casey sees Ireland as a dying country—weakened and made pale by church influence; a country which he feels has broken the stranglehold of the lion and the unicorn only to be suffocated by the cross and the shamrock.

O'Casey: There's a book that was recently censored in Ireland—*Kings, Lords, and Commons*—it contains a translation of the finest Gaelic—a beautiful Gaelic poem,[2] by Frank O'Connor. He translated these poems from the Gaelic and most of them are really beautiful; but the Gaelic writers are much freer in talk and much bolder in expression than the Irish writers in English, and there are in a number of them certain passages that wouldn't be tolerated by the present-day Irish writers because of the fear of the church, but they're boldly stated in the Gaelic, and, of course, hardly any of the Bishops know any of the Gaelic, so they are utterly ignorant of the contents of this book in Gaelic—but they immediately condemned and banned it when it appeared in English; and then they tell us that England, Ireland and the rest of the free nations are determined to defend freedom withal, and here's an instance of a book in Gaelic—our national tongue, Ireland's national tongue—banned by the Irish themselves. How, then, can you blame any intellectual or any man that's determined, that is intelligent, that is determined to speak freely about anything that he's interested in—how can you expect him to stay in a country like that? He has to get out of it and come to tolerant England, or tolerant United States, where, at least, he'll be able to say many more things than he could possibly say in Ireland, although he's not able to say everything either in England or the United States that he might wish to say. I wrote a play once called *The Star Turns Red*, not a very good play, but it has one very fine scene in it. Well, that was submitted to the then Lord Chamberlain and he said no, he wouldn't allow this to be produced—he didn't like the theme. Well, I didn't expect him to like the theme, I didn't

2. 'The Midnight Court', c. 1790 by Brian Merriman.

wish anybody else to like the theme if they so desired. A person has a perfect right to dislike a thing as much as he has a right to like it, but I don't select my themes to please the Lord Chamberlain—I write plays to please myself.

Webster: Whatever the facts of the situation are, when we are faced with O'Casey's opinions, we are faced with O'Casey. His plays and his opinions form an unusual oneness. His beliefs have been painfully formed on the anvil of his own life and the expression of his opinion guided by his conscience alone. He has a strong intuitive awareness of right and wrong, which echoes massively through the last scene of his great tapestry of human suffering, *Juno and the Paycock*:

Mrs Boyle: I forgot, Mary, I forgot; your poor oul' selfish mother brother, an' me to see me poor dead son!

Mary: I dhread it, mother, I dhread it!

Mrs Boyle: I forgot, Mary, I forgot; your poor oul' selfish mother was only thinkin' of herself. No, no, you mustn't come—it wouldn't be good for you. You go on to me sisther's an' I'll face th' ordeal meself. Maybe I didn't feel sorry enough for Mrs Tancred when her poor son was found as Johnny's been found now— because he was a Diehard! Ah, why didn't I remember that then he wasn't a Diehard or a Stater, but only a poor dead son! It's well I remember all that she said—an' it's my turn to say it now: What was the pain I suffered, Johnny, bringin' you into the world to carry you to your cradle, to the pains I'll suffer carryin' you out o' the world to bring you to your grave! Mother o' God, Mother o' God, have pity on us all! Blessed Virgin, where were you when me darlin' son was riddled with bullets, when me darlin' son was riddled with bullets? Sacred Heart o' Jesus, take away our hearts o' stone, and give us hearts o' flesh! Take away this murdherin' hate, an' give us Thine own eternal love!

[*They all go slowly out.*
[*There is a pause; then a sound of shuffling steps on the stairs outside. The door opens and Boyle and Joxer, both of them very drunk, enter.*

Boyle: I'm able to go no farther. . . . Two polis, ey . . . what were they doin' here, I wondher? . . . Up to no good, anyhow . . . an' Juno an' that lovely daughter o' mine with them. [*Taking a sixpence from his pocket and looking at it*] Wan single, solitary tanner left out of all I borreyed. . . . [*He lets it fall.*] The last o' the Mohicans. . . . The blinds is down, Joxer, the blinds is down!

Joxer [*walking unsteadily across the room, and anchoring at the bed*]: Put all . . . your throubles . . . in your oul' kit-bag . . . an' smile . . . smile . . . smile!

Boyle: The counthry'll have to steady itself . . . it's goin' . . . to hell. . . . Where'r all . . . the chairs . . . gone to . . . steady itself, Joxer. . . . Chairs'll . . . have to . . . steady themselves. . . . No matther . . . what any one may . . . say. . . . Irelan' sober . . . is Irelan' . . . free.

Joxer [*stretching himself on the bed*]: Chains . . . an' . . slaveree . . . that's a darlin' motto . . . a daaarlin' . . . motto!

Boyle: If th' worst comes . . . to th' worse . . . I can join a . . . flyin' . . . column. . . . I done . . . me bit . . . in Easther Week . . . had no business . . . to . . . be . . . there . . . but Captain Boyle's Captain Boyle!

Joxer: Breathes there a man with soul . . . so . . . de . . . ad . . . this . . . me . . . o . . . wn, me nat . . . ive l . . . an'!

Boyle [*subsiding into a sitting posture on the floor*]: Commandant Kelly died . . . in them . . . arms . . . Joxer. . . . Tell me Volunteer Butties . . . says he . . . that . . . I died for . . . Irelan'!

Joxer: D'jever rade Willie . . . Reilly . . . an' his own . . . Colleen . . . Bawn? It's a darlin' story, a daarlin' story!

Boyle: I'm telling you . . . Joxer . . . th' whole worl's . . . in a terr . . . ible state o' . . . chassis!

Webster: Through this darkness and despair, the young O'Casey, many years ago, saw the gleam of a richer colour and grasped it to him and has held tightly to it ever since. The song in the sigh, the red roses in the dark.

O'Casey [*intones softly*]:

A sober black shawl hides her body entirely,
Touch'd be th' sun an' th' salt spray of th' sea;
But down in th' darkness a slim hand, so lovely,
Carries a rich bunch of red roses for me!

O'Casey and Ireland*

'Why shouldn't Ireland get into the Soviet bloc? She'd be more secure there.' The trenchancy of the remark will leave no doubt who made it. When I spoke to Sean O'Casey at his home in Torquay, it was obvious that, in spite of an illness that has lasted eight weeks, his mind had lost none of its liveliness. 'I am not an angel yet,' he said, and went on to show that he is keeping very much in touch with this world by talking about Ireland's application to join the Common Market.

The idea that Ireland might go into NATO obviously appalled him. 'But Ireland has been changing a lot and you'll be pushed in. I can't understand why you don't set up an embassy or a chargé d'affaires with the Soviet Union which was the first country to recognise the Republic. It is stupid to ignore her and you could get a good market for your bacon and butter there.'

Schools too were very much on his mind. 'Did you see what the headmaster of Rugby said about the Soviet schools when he was there recently? He could never have said it about the British schools, let alone the Irish ones. I get a lot of letters from Irish people complaining about the way children are treated in the schools. Some of the things I have been told are brutal.'

*   *   *

As for writing, he told me that he did not tell people what he was doing. 'I am trying to write,' he told me. 'But I spend a lot of the day reading the *Irish Times*, *Focus*, the *Daily Worker*, and various Soviet and Chinese magazines and newspapers. And I spend quite a lot of time answering letters.'

Asked whether he intended to go to Ireland, he said: 'I'll never go to Ireland again. At 82 one doesn't care to travel. But some day the oul' soul might fly to Leinster House to have a look at the *Dail*.' [1] I told him that his soul would probably find it depressing. 'What do you mean?' he said. 'Have you never been in the House of Com-

---

* *Irish Times* (Dublin), 3 March, 1962, p. 9, originally entitled 'London Letter: "O'Casey Speaks"'.

1. The Irish Parliament.

mons?' But it was clear that the chief thing he was thinking about was blocs and divisions between people. 'It is nonsense to talk about this bloc, and that bloc, and the other. Everyone will have to get together some time.'

I mentioned Elizabeth Coxhead's book about Lady Gregory, and he said that he had heard she was writing one [2] about Maud Gonne. 'But why doesn't somebody Irish write about these people? Are they all envious of what they did?' He said that he had no intention of allowing a play of his to be put on at the Abbey. 'The Abbey died when Yeats died,' he said. 'The standard of acting and production are ruined, and everything you see there now is rubbish. The last time I was in the Abbey was in 1935,[3] when I was in Dublin with my wife, and we saw *Candida*. But they don't produce plays there any more.' Listening to the crusty Dublin voice, it was evident that however long O'Casey has been in Devon, he has never lost his love for and interest in Ireland.

2. *Daughters of Erin* (London, 1965), a study of Irish feminist leaders.
3. Shortly after the Abbey had finally staged *The Silver Tassie*, on 12 August, 1935.

O'Casey and the Critic*

NIALL CARROLL †

Up to the early sixties all my dealings with O'Casey were in the published open-letter form of comment and reply. I had never met or spoken to him on the telephone. In all the circumstances I didn't particularly want to, but that day came when I had to face the music. As I have suggested here, it is an old trick of the newspaper world to telephone a big name—we did it many times with Shaw—and needle him into making a worthwhile comment.

One day *Sunday Press* News Editor, Gerry Fox, showed me the London Letter of the *Irish Times*, in which O'Casey was quoted as saying that the Abbey nowadays produced only rubbish and pro-

* Extracted from Sean McCann (ed.), *The World of Sean O'Casey* (London: The New English Library, Four Square Books, 1966), 'The Bonfire', pp. 134-6.
† Drama critic of the *Irish Press*, and playwright.

duced it in rubbishy fashion. He suggested I telephone O'Casey and remind him he had not been in Dublin for over thirty years—and was this just hearsay? It was too good an opportunity to let go, so I took several deep breaths and called his number in Torquay. I trembled a little as I heard his 'hello'. I told him I was speaking for the *Sunday Press* and before I could say any more he said gruffly: 'I don't know anything about the *Sunday Press*. What do they want with me?'

I said: 'They're interested in a statement attributed to you in the press about the poor standard of present-day Abbey plays and production. They know you haven't been in Ireland since the early thirties and are puzzled that you would express opinions founded on hearsay.'

He had been quietly belligerent up to this but the reaction to my query was instantaneous. I might say he erupted like a volcano.

'Hearsay?' he roared, as I instinctively held the receiver a few inches away from my ear. 'It's no hearsay. I know what's going on over there. I am in close touch. I know more about the Abbey and Dublin and Ireland than you and the *Sunday Press* that are on the spot.'

I felt myself disintegrating but the certainty that a magnificent half-column of copy would be the reward helped to bolster my courage.

'It's just that we find it strange to have someone like you talking at secondhand in such a direct way,' I managed to say.

'Secondhand?' he roared again. Then he paused suddenly and said: 'I don't like to be talking to mysterious distant voices. Who are you?'

The images of *The Bishop's Bonfire*, *The Green Crow*, *Father Ned* and Owen Keegan all floated wraithfully past me in the terrible moment of truth. Brazenly as I thought, but I felt my voice dry and hoarse, I gave him my name.

I heard the slow, deliberate intake of breath over the line and then the long-drawn-out Ohhhhhh. . . . The silence which followed seemed never-ending. But when he spoke again his voice had undergone a complete transformation. It was soft, no anger in it at all but a slight note of paternal chiding:

'You said a great many foolish things in your time, didn't you son?'

Considering the tone and the comment and recalling years of

wordy battles between Dublin and Devon, what was one to say in answer? I tried to convey to him that my own generation were too young to have seen the rejection of his first great plays, that they felt they could not enthuse over his later works but had done their utmost to undo the wrongs of the twenties and early thirties in his own regard. He grudgingly admitted that Ireland now received his first plays with special warmth but would not concede that his later plays were any less meritorious.

His anger now completely gone, except when he mentioned the Abbey, he talked quietly about life in the newspapers and asked me if I was a full-time journalist. I told him I was and he said: 'Yes, I am a journalist too. We're all journalists, we writers. We interpret the world for others. That's our job.'

Then as if regretting his first outburst on the telephone, he told me: 'I read everything about Ireland in the newspapers and I'm always meeting people coming here from Dublin. There's nothing goes on across the Irish Sea that I don't know about. As a matter of fact I know all about your tide that wouldn't come in or wouldn't go out, down where you come from.'

To my horror he was referring to my Abbey comedy, *The Wanton Tide*, produced shortly before.

He was in great talking form and I knew I was meeting an entirely new Sean O'Casey.

Suddenly he said: 'You know, you ought to be ashamed of yourself to ring me up and talk in English.' He thereupon broke into fluent Irish and insisted that I use it also, so I struggled to keep up the conversation in the medium. I told him, in Irish, that I had learned to speak the language in Galway but that when I came to Dublin I had no opportunity to speak it and had forgotten a great deal of it.

'No excuse at all,' said O'Casey. 'Look at me. I make opportunities to speak Irish all the time with my family and with the people who call to see me from Ireland.'

There was more talk on minor everyday matters and then O'Casey sighed heavily and said: 'Ah yes, the Abbey . . . I wouldn't ever touch that crowd again.' I felt him sitting up straight in his chair as he said suddenly: 'Do you know the quotation—"*Romantic Ireland's dead and gone, it's with O'Leary in the grave*"?'

'It's Yeats,' I said.

'Well, I'll paraphrase it for you,' said O'Casey. ' "The Abbey

Theatre's dead and gone, it's with Yeats in his grave". So long, son.'
There was a click as the receiver was replaced.

It was over and I felt better than I had ever felt in my life. I had spoken to Sean O'Casey who could at a moment's notice shed all the harsh qualities of character we had all been accustomed to debit him with and become a gentle human being exuding only humour, kindliness and goodwill.

It was a relief to know that there really were two Sean O'Caseys and a treat indeed to meet the second one.

The Sting and the Twinkle*

W. J. WEATHERBY †

Everyone encountered in Torquay seemed to know a local resident by the name of Sean O'Casey but not many knew his work. Several people who gave elaborate directions as to the whereabouts of his home cooed at the very mention of his name, as Londoners do when you mention Buckingham Palace. 'He's a great gentleman,' said a man gently mowing his lawn with a machine that badly needed some oil. He stopped mowing when he learnt that the great gentleman was also a great writer even though his works were not seen on television. 'Fancy that!' he said and went inside to tell his wife.

London knows this side of him, grudgingly admitting his greatness even while it neglected him, but it has not caught up with the man Torquay knows. It still clings to that old illusion that he is a cranky, bitter, Irishman—a 'flying wasp' as he once called himself. But—with a London festival of O'Casey plays opening at the Mermaid Theatre [1]—this is surely a good time to put the whole man together—the great (as London might say) and the good (as Torquay would call him).

Both are on view over afternoon tea. The only handicap for a

---

* *Manchester Guardian*, 15 August, 1962, p. 7. Also in *Irish Times* (Dublin), 15 August, 1962, p. 8.
† See note on p. 103.

1. *Purple Dust, Red Roses for Me, The Plough and the Stars* (15 August–13 October, 1962).

s.t.—5**

reporter is that the O'Casey words do not tell all—he can make a waspish remark and then take away the sting with a twinkle. Perhaps the London that has neglected him caught the sting and Torquay has learnt to see the twinkle.

'Sean is resting. He will be up presently,' said Mrs O'Casey, the beautiful Eileen, the heroine of his work. She will be representing him at the festival—the perfect O'Casey ambassador. With them at present is his American biographer, Dr David Krause, who is preparing a collection of O'Casey letters [2] which may stretch into three volumes by the time he has run them to earth in several countries. Soon the prolific letter writer himself appeared. Outwardly there was no change since I last saw him two years ago. He even sat in the same seat facing the Augustus John portrait of him and looking now like the wise old father of the fierce, proud young man John painted.

'There has been a change,' he said, taking off his glasses. 'My eyes have almost gone now. The most aggravating thing is I can't read in bed when I'm ill and that's terrible because I hate bed. Still I've had them for eighty-three years and they were pretty bad when I was five years of age. I'm not whining about it. It's just that I'm passionately fond of reading. I'm planning to buy records of Shakespeare's plays so if I can't read them I can hear them.'

He put on his glasses again and sought and successfully found his pipe. 'I love poking my nose in flowers and I can still see the colour if I get close enough. I'm also very fond of birds and now the damn things won't wait for me to get close enough to see them. Brooks Atkinson—you know, the former drama critic of the *New York Times*—is writing a book on birds and he asked me if I remembered any little incidents about them. So I sent him a letter about the first time I saw the swallows and the first time I saw a young cuckoo.' [3]

'Tea's ready, children,' announced Mrs O'Casey, appearing at the door of the sitting room.

'You know Yeats didn't have a five pound note until he was over forty. He told me that himself,' said Mr O'Casey, settling himself at the dining table after dipping his head close to the bowl of flowers near his plate. 'The only hope for the young Irish writers since this bloody England left after persecuting and torturing and hanging us —the only thing for them is to go to that blasted country which persecuted them!'

2. Not yet published.
3. *New York Times*, 4 September, 1962, p. 30.

'You mean the English ruling class of the time persecuted the Irish—'

The bright eyes peered over the table. 'Are you a Socialist by any chance? There's always a ruling class. I had a strong dislike of the English people because I thought them all scoundrels until I met them. They were lads from the Buckinghamshire and Warwickshire Regiment brought over to put down the rebellion—young country lads of seventeen or eighteen terrified of what they were going to do, of the dangers and of death. I saw they were no different from our lads; they were very kindly except in danger when they shot away at any damn thing. We all looked forward to the Tommies coming because they were kindly. The people in the tenement houses used to make tea for them. It was the Black and Tans we hated—most of them were brutal ruffians, though even some in the auxiliary were fine men.'

He took off his glasses. 'Do you think Marilyn Monroe would have died if we had had socialism? Who killed Marilyn Monroe—that's a question. That was a tragedy that affected me very much. I hate the idea of Hollywood in which she had to survive. She said she wanted to meet me when she was over here and I wish I had. I would have liked to have talked with her.'

'Perhaps you could have helped her, dear,' said Mrs O'Casey.

'Sometimes someone can help another person. Who knows? It's so easy to be foolish and so hard to be wise. I never knew she had such a hard upbringing—all those foster homes, never a real home.'

'It was incredible that it didn't make her hard and bitter—'

'Oh,' said Mr O'Casey. 'Bitterness is no good to you. You only lose if you're bitter.'

He led the way from the table to his study, where he lay back on a couch to rest his back and light his pipe. 'I didn't select the plays for the festival. Bernard Miles did that. I have no preference except possibly *The Silver Tassie* and *Cock-a-Doodle Dandy*. My favourite is always what I'm doing at the moment. I've just corrected the galley proofs of a collection of essays.[4] I shan't be able to do another play until I work out whether I can write into a tape recorder or not. Eileen's really my eyes now.

'You know when I wrote *Purple Dust*, James Agate rushed into print and called me all kinds of names and said that I had stabbed England in the back. That was an extraordinary thing to say—that

4. *Under a Colored Cap* (1963).

the two men in the play represented England, a country of fifty million people, the miners, the dockers, the railwaymen, the clerical union, teachers, doctors—they're all England. Agate was a bit out of touch—like Asquith with whom I once dined.'

'Did you write Asquith any letters?' inquired Dr Krause.

'No, he wasn't my kind of man. Very nice. A classical scholar. But out of touch with the life of the people.'

He took his glasses off again. 'I haven't lifted the ban on my plays in Ireland. Except for Bernard Miles—he can take the festival plays there if he wants to. A kind of hail and farewell. The ban anyway can only apply to professional productions because 35 years ago I was very poor and had to sell my amateur rights for a lump sum. But there will be no professional productions otherwise. I'm still very bitter about their failure to stand up against that Roman Catholic Archbishop [5] who didn't like my play. . . .'

'Are you in favour of the national theatre?'

'Of course. England ought to have one. There's hardly a country in the world that hasn't—but I'm really much more in favour of municipal theatres. Every town with over 15,000 people should have one. Sir Laurence Olivier ought to be a good director. It's a glorious way for him to end his life.'

'He's only about 55,' said Mrs O'Casey.

'Thirty years [6] isn't a long time to be in charge of a national theatre. There are so many things to be done. That would make him 85, even older than I am. I hope it won't be confined to the Elizabethans. It must be very different from Stratford. It should have room for all the continentals—plays from all the countries of the world.'

'Plus a couple of plays of ours, love,' said Mrs O'Casey with a smile.

'I wouldn't have any objection to that. I would like to see Synge done. Then the O'Neill cycle and Thornton Wilder. I would like to see a Negro play there. There are thousands of plays that should be done, but I suppose they will go on the old conventional lines, producing Shakespeare and *Lady Windermere's Fan*.

He puffed on his pipe and then took off his glasses again. 'Do you

5. Most Rev. Dr J. McQuaid—one of the most powerful and conservative figures in Ireland who wielded considerable influence behind the political scenes and was said to be largely responsible for the banning of many books, plays and films of recognised intellectual quality.

6. Olivier resigned from the directorship in 1973 after ten years.

believe in life after death?' he asked suddenly. 'I can't. I would like to because I have so many loved ones that are gone and I would like to meet them again. Then there's George Bernard Shaw, Shakespeare and the whole damn lot—you'd never get bored for a thousand years. But I can't believe it. I have tried but I can't. I can't see any evidence that points to it.'

He was lost behind a cloud of smoke and when he emerged again he looked tired—tired enough for his visitors to retire. He put on his glasses again to see us out.

The Green Crow in Devon*

BROOKS ATKINSON †

If it were in Sean O'Casey's nature to feel doleful about anything, he would have ample reason.

He is thin and frail. At the age of 83 he has no vision in one eye and very little in the other. He has a spinal infirmity that compels him to lie on the couch in his study a good part of the time.

But nothing depresses the humorous spirit of this indomitable Irish writer, who lives with his indomitable wife, Eileen, in the second floor flat of a suburban house on a hill.

He looks gay. To ward off winter draughts, he wears an embroidered skull cap, which makes him look a little like a chief rabbi, and a red house robe, which makes him look a little like a giddy bishop. Altogether an odd but lively figure as he gropes his way around the room. Smoking Erinmore tobacco in a worn pipe, peering amiably through metal-framed glasses with his one usable eye, he gives an impression of enjoying life and knowing a lot about it in terms of experience, history, religion, art, and theatre literature.

In a new book of essays, to be entitled *Under a Colored Cap*, he will denounce what he regards as W. H. Auden's dismal view of life.

* *New York Times*, 31 December, 1962, p. 5, originally entitled 'Visit With Sean O'Casey: Despite Infirmities, The Green Crow is Still in Good Form'.

† Theatre critic of the *New York Times* for thirty years, joining the staff of that paper in 1925. Has written numerous books on the American theatre. Edited *The Sean O'Casey Reader: Plays, Autobiographies, Opinions* (London: Macmillan; New York: St Martin's Press, 1968).

'Life has never been futile for me,' Mr O'Casey observed. 'Of course, there's been a lot of pain in it, but that's a part of it, and I've also enjoyed the fights I have been in.' The manuscript of the new book has been examined by his publisher's prudent solicitor. A few cautious suggestions have been made. One that Mr O'Casey regrets acceding to is an impertinent sentence in an essay [1] about Kenneth Tynan, drama critic of *The Observer*.

Within the past few years Mr Tynan has had the effrontery to disparage some O'Casey work and make at least one factual error. No man to take anything lying down, Mr O'Casey wrote: '*Mr Tynan has a very bad habit of running too fast in front of his own nose.*' Mr O'Casey is sorry to lose a phrase he is fond of.[2] But he does not want to distress his publishers who have been loyal to him for almost forty years. 'I guess I'm softening up,' he said with a wry grin.

Because of his grievously impaired vision, he finds it difficult to write. Eileen ('God bless her!') helps him as much as she can. But he has to hold his work within a few inches of the one eye that still gives a little vision. If he is interrupted, it takes him ten or fifteen minutes to find the place where he left off. He is working on the script of a film that John Whiting,[3] a British playwright, has made from the first three volumes of the O'Casey autobiography—*I Knock at the Door, Pictures in the Hallway* and *Inishfallen, Fare Thee Well*. The film will be entitled *Young Cassidy*.

But Mr O'Casey is unhappy because the text does not use the original dialogue. Out of professional respect for another writer's work, he does not like to tamper with Mr Whiting's text. But in the laborious scrawl of a man who is nearly blind, Mr O'Casey is slowly introducing some of his own dialogue.

Since he has picked many fights and fought valiantly in others, he has a public reputation for combativeness. Essentially, Mr O'Casey is a modest, warm-hearted man with a cheerful soul. He is always surprised when people take offence at his thunderbolts. A few years ago he felt that the archbishop of the Roman Catholic church in Dublin had insulted Joyce and himself by refusing to offer a votive mass at a festival in which their works were scheduled to appear. Mr O'Casey angrily banned the professional use of his works in Ireland. For several years they have been performed only by amateurs.

1. *Under a Colored Cap*, 'Purple Dust in their Eyes', pp. 261–77.
2. But he used the phrase in a letter (1 October, 1962) to John O'Riordan.
3. Author of *The Devils, Marching Song*, and other plays.

Although he is still smarting from an old insult, he does not regard the ban as inflexible and may reconsider it for a future Dublin theatre festival.

Although he is full of years and infirmities he is alert and optimistic, with a relish of anything comic. In the winter, the grass is still green in Torquay, and people still work in their kitchen gardens. Although Mr O'Casey is no longer able to see the green woodpecker who visits an old tree in the garden, he enjoys hearing him tap, and he listens to the tawny owl in the evening. The Green Crow, as he once described himself, is in good form. Although his voice is soft, it is spirited.

Tea with Sean*

JOHN O'RIORDAN †

On my way to the annual weekend conference of the Association of Assistant Librarians held at Newton Abbot, I telephoned the Torquay home of Sean O'Casey.

Over the earpiece came a rich Dublin accent reminiscent of Shaw's. 'Would that be Mr O'Riordan?' His note of caution prompted by his dislike of certain writers and newspapers, was followed by: 'You may come to tea . . . don't talk to me of your honours and privileges . . . I'll expect you at quarter-to-five.'

The visit, if not pre-arranged, was not unexpected. I had corresponded with the playwright a few times since the O'Casey Festival was staged at the Mermaid Theatre in London last year.

At 83, with strength ebbing out of him, and his eyesight nearly gone, this remarkable Irishman is still active in the spheres of literature and the theatre, even though he remains unfashionable and unpopular—living in exile among the quiet Devon hills, shunning

* *Enfield Weekly Herald*, 19 April, 1963, p. 4 (by permission of North London Weekly Herald Newspapers Ltd). Also extracted in *Enfield Gazette and Observer*, 31 May, 1963, p. 7.

† One of the editors of the present book. Literary Adviser in London to Eileen O'Casey. Articles and reviews on O'Casey in *Tribune* (London) and *Library Review* (Glasgow). Public Librarian of Southgate, London, N.14, with the London Borough of Enfield.

all forms of publicity and refusing time and time again to go on either
television or radio.

From Babbacombe Downs, high up above sea level overlooking
a glorious sweep of Devon coastline, the road led to the O'Caseys'
home at St Marychurch.

Mrs O'Casey, the beautiful Eileen, devoted wife and heroine of
his work, opened the door and said, 'Sean is expecting you. He has
been resting. He will be here in a minute.'

Their upstairs flat, not far from the reach of the coast, was taste-
fully decorated and crammed with books and pictures.

Presently Sean appeared, clad in a red gown and soft felt slippers,
and wearing a coloured cloth skull cap—evidently to give the old
rebel an air of respectability. He peered at me from behind thick,
steel-rimmed spectacles, looking at once like an old leprechaun and
yet, at the same time, like an aged priest.

In two memorable hours I was regaled with crackling phrases—
excitingly like the dialogue of his plays (natural talk, as only the
Irish know how, and tinged with O'Casey colour).

*   *   *

No one, he said, who hadn't in him 'a quivering fibre of poetry'
could hope to write a fine play, and many of today's plays—whether
on television or in the West End—were nothing more than 'fledgling,
apprentice work'. 'They strut the stage for a thousand-and-one
nights, but when the last night of their performance comes and the
curtain falls, they fall, too; like Lucifer, never to hope again.'

Hadn't Liam O'Flaherty written himself out? And Brendan
Behan—he didn't think he had it in him to be a great dramatist.

I asked, teasingly, if he had seen the father of the Behan family
on the television programme, 'This is Your Life'. 'I don't often watch
television, because of my eyes, and from inclination as well, but I
did on that occasion. A vulgar, bloody man. No credit to the Irish.
Even Eamonn Andrews looked dumbfounded!'

His talk wandered round the universe from Shaw and James
Joyce to Barry Fitzgerald—'Poor Barry, he was the only actor I
really loved.' [1] Ambition, he believed, was the curse of present-day
life. 'I don't care what your creed or colour is, so long as you take
your fill of life and live it to the full.'

He spoke about his new book just published—*Under a Colored*

1. Barry Fitzgerald died in 1961.

Cap—which, explained his wife, represented a lifetime's impressions of such controversial topics as religion and politics, as well as a selection of some of his finest essays, verses and autobiographical pieces, together with pungent comments on literature and the drama today and a refutation of hostile criticisms hurled at him by 'ignorant, foolish critics'.

*   *   *

His talk changed to Ireland and the Irish. 'My first love, of course, is with the Irish people.' A pause, and then the quick, thin smile that is never far from his lips. 'But they don't seem to appreciate me very much.'

He spoke of his own family and grandchildren, and asked me about my wife, Kathleen, and small son, Vincent—whom, of course, he has not seen—as if, like the rest of humanity they belonged to him.

He, himself, was the thirteenth child of a family of thirteen living in a Dublin slum tenement, and eight of those children died in childhood. Today, he is the only one left—but, undoubtedly, the greatest of them all.

A truly great celebrity, and both kindly and considerate as well. No stage Irishman this, but one born almost out of his time. His writings have enriched the world and his fame will endure.

A Great 'Hurrah' for Life*

JACK LEVETT

In 1964, O'Casey gave permission for the Abbey Theatre Company to perform *Juno and the Paycock* [1] in London, and I asked him why?

'The reason is plain enough. They want to perform it as part of the Shakespeare celebrations [2]—and I could never refuse Shakespeare anything.

'Why, there's more social understanding in Shakespeare than in all

* Extracted from *Daily Worker* (London), 30 March, 1964, p. 2.

1. As well as *The Plough and the Stars*, at the Aldwych Theatre (21 April–2 May, 1964), as part of the first World Theatre Season.
2. In honour of the 400th anniversary of Shakespeare's birth.

the Labour leaders rolled into one big ball. All some of them think about now is how soon they can get into the House of Lords.

'Now it's Lord Willis, wearing his ermine robes so that he can look like the rest of 'em. How can any self-respecting Socialist dress himself like that to prance about in a monkey-house? They should be fighting to abolish it—should have abolished it when they had the power to.

'I've more bitterness now about things—the poverty and misery that still exist around us—than I ever had.'

The future concerns O'Casey now as much as it did in his youth. His last volume of autobiography, *Sunset and Evening Star*, concludes with a great 'Hurrah!' for life— to all it had been, to what it was, to what it would be.

And what it will be, for the peoples of the world, is still in O'Casey's mind at the age of 84.

O'Casey's vision was put clearly by the strike-leader Ayamonn, in his great play about the 1913 strike, *Red Roses for Me*:

Fair city, I tell thee that children's white laughter,
An' all th' red joy of grave youth goin' gay,
Shall make of thy streets a wild harp ever sounding,
Touch'd by th' swift fingers of young ones at play!

We swear to release thee from hunger an' hardship,
From things that are ugly an' common an' mean;
Thy people together shall build a brave city,
Th' fairest an' finest that ever was seen!

Ayamonn's fair city is Dublin, but O'Casey's is the world. And when we build it, he, as much as any man, will have made it possible.

A Modest Proposal*

ANGUS DRUMMOND

'I've never regarded myself as an angry young man or an angry old man,' remarked Sean O'Casey. 'I don't think I'm either. I've no particular anger, old or young.'

His work has been, to him, his all.

In 1955, when *The Bishop's Bonfire* had its première in Dublin, he was asked: 'Is it comedy or tragedy?'

'Sure,' he replied, 'it's like life itself, a bit of both.'

A few days later, invited to comment on the boos and catcalls which greeted the final curtain of the first night at the Gaiety Theatre, he said: 'Several of my plays have had similar receptions in London and other places as well as Dublin. If nothing else, it makes sure that they don't get overlooked although, of course, only certain sections of the audience are so demonstrative.'

'I have no favourites,' he said in 1962, when asked if he approved of the plays chosen for an O'Casey festival at the Mermaid Theatre. 'The only favourite I have is whatever I happen to be doing at the moment.'

Sometimes he digressed wildly, as when he recalled passing a graveyard during a stroll—'They're depressing, atrocious and unhygienic. Councils should turn them into children's play parks. That would be a far better use for the land.'

And his happy hunting ground?

'Anywhere in the world where they put on my plays is a happy hunting ground for me.'

* Extracted from *Courier* (London), **42**, no. 4 (April, 1964), pp. 40–1, originally published as 'O'Casey Says'.

'Abbey has been Deteriorating for Years,' says Sean O'Casey*

JOHN HOWARD

Sean O'Casey had not read the statement from the Abbey Theatre directors when I spoke to him, and he was not interested in it. 'There's no need to read it to me,' he said. 'I can guess what they said. They probably said: "How could O'Casey know anything about it?"'

He said that he did not need to see the Abbey production at the Aldwych Theatre to give an opinion about it. 'I judge from the world around me. I can see things and understand things and give opinions about things without seeing them. It is a well-known fact for years now that the Abbey has deteriorated. Who is going to say it has not? It has been going on for years.

'Years ago a public protest was made from the audience against the quality of the production and acting in *The Plough and the Stars*. About a week before the Abbey Company went to London a serious article appeared in the monthly magazine, *Focus*, and the writer actually suggested that they should be prevented from going because of the inferior quality of the production. Why didn't the Abbey directors exclaim against this article?'

Mr O'Casey went on to say that many visitors to Ireland dropped in to see him when they came to Britain and they all said that the Abbey was a sorry spectacle.[1]

*   *   *

'What the hell does Blythe know about the drama, anyway?' O'Casey asked. 'He knows nothing about acting or drama. He may be a good manager in a financial sense but he doesn't understand the drama. I have a letter from him in which he condemns himself. He says they weed out a number of plays that have been submitted until they have about ten left. Then they read these again and select

* *Irish Times* (Dublin), 4 July, 1964, pp. 1, 11.

1. Similar views were expressed by the actor and director, Jack MacGowran (interview), *The Times* (London), 18 March, 1967, p. 7.

two or three which they consider to be the best and they finally select the one they think will fill the house. That is no way for a national theatre to select a play. They neglect what they think would be a better play if they think it would not make money.

'It doesn't matter if I was at the Aldwych or not. They had to get three of the old troupers—Eileen Crowe, May Craig and Eric Gorman —to play three very important parts. Why had they to do that if the quality of the acting in the present company is so fine as Mr Blythe and the other directors make out? If they are producing such fine actors why had they to get a man of over 80 and a woman of 70 to take over these parts? Will the directors answer that?'

O'Casey seemed in great form as we spoke and before finishing he said he would like to tell people to go to the Abbey and judge for themselves.

'One last thing . . . it has not been pleasant to have to say these things about the Abbey. I would love to see the Abbey the finest company in the world. That is my feeling.'

Mr Blythe, when asked about O'Casey's charge that in a letter to the playwright he had said that they eventually chose a play that they thought would fill the house, and therefore chose plays for their money potential, commented:

'That is entirely wrong. We never reject a play on the basis that it may not make money, when we find that it is a good play. If we think that a play is good we give it a chance whether we feel it would fill the house or not. But we *do* recall plays that have filled the house and we do *not* recall plays that have not. That is a different thing. It would be senseless to recall a play that has proved it will not make money and that the public have rejected. I may add that if there is a good play that we think will not fill the house at its first presentation, we may not put it on immediately, but eventually we *will* put it on.'

*   *   *

A statement issued by the directors of the Abbey Theatre indicated that 'The directors of the Abbey Theatre have read with great interest Mr Sean O'Casey's announcement that they have been dead for years. They would like to assure Mr O'Casey that, as in the case of Mark Twain, the rumour is greatly exaggerated. Dead men tell no tales, not even that of *Juno* or *Plough* or *Gunman*.

Mr O'Casey's statement that the directors know nothing about acting or the Drama is patently absurd. The long-standing involvement of each of them in various aspects of the work of the Theatre is common knowledge.

'As to Mr O'Casey's reference to the managing director, the point is that his relationship with the board is precisely that of the managing director of any ordinary business establishment, except that the directors of the Abbey Theatre have always taken a bigger share of control of its work than is customary in a commercial concern. In particular, they have always retained control of the two most important functions in the theatre, the acceptance and selection of plays, and the assessment of the producer's casting proposals.

'In spite of differences of opinion with Mr O'Casey, the directors share his enthusiasm for the idea of making the Abbey Theatre the best in the world, and all their efforts are directed towards that end.'

O'Casey and the Press*

AIDAN HENNIGAN †

Although I had visited his home at Torquay, the close friendship I had with Sean O'Casey was really developed over the phone.

It started more or less when he roundly abused me for ringing him early one morning. After my stammered apologies he asked me, 'Are you courting?' and when I said I was he replied, 'God help the poor girl. It will be another Irish romance, twenty years I suppose.'

Often when I rang him afterwards he would answer the phone and say, 'This is the gardener speaking—what do you want O'Casey for?' or 'O'Casey does not want to speak to anyone'.

After this outburst all I had to do was to wait a little while and he came back again. 'O'Casey cannot be bothered talking to any of the Irish papers or for that matter to anyone in Ireland.'

Invariably this was the introduction to a long conversation and once started O'Casey would talk non-stop for as long as twenty minutes on subjects ranging from the Abbey Theatre to Communism, from writing to television.

In later years many had thought of O'Casey as an irascible, rather

---

* From Sean McCann (ed.), *The World of Sean O'Casey*, pp. 179–80.
† See note on p. 115.

bitter old man. This was far from the truth, at least as far as my own personal experience went. Often, at the height of a tirade directed at the Abbey Theatre, I would say to him, 'You are being a bit hard, aren't you?' and he would laugh with infectious good humour and reply: 'I love to have a go and shake them up.'

And for all his criticisms of Irish institutions he was remarkably keen to find out what was happening at home. I never had a conversation with him in which he did not ask many, many questions about every facet of Irish life.

A point he often made to me was that work was the only answer to anyone's problems. 'Of course,' he would add, 'I have to work—O'Casey is not a rich man you know.'

There are many things I remember about O'Casey. He was not overfond of newspapermen, and I believe he heartily disliked critics. But once you gained his confidence he would talk without hesitation.

When *Juno and the Paycock* and *The Plough and the Stars* were being produced in the Aldwych Theatre for the World Theatre series he asked me to go along and to tell him what they were like.

I made the mistake of replying that the critics would give a more objective view. It was the first time I heard O'Casey really mad on the phone. I managed to catch words like 'phonies', 'hell', 'damnation' and a few other unprintable adjectives.

When Brendan Behan died [1] O'Casey was very moved. He spoke about the tragedy of Behan's drinking and the great talent that had been killed.

My impression of the later O'Casey was that despite his crusty exterior he was a kindly man bearing as best he could the infirmities of his years. I think too he had tremendous humanity.

1. In 1964, aged 41.

Tea and Memories and Songs at a Last Fond Visit*

GJON MILI †

Stepping out of the car—it was just two months ago—I heard Eileen O'Casey's voice, 'He's here, my dear, he's here.' I raised my eyes and stopped. There at the top of the stairs stood Sean with his arms outstretched, like a tree with two branches. 'Is it you,lad?' he said, 'Is it you? I don't see very well now. In fact I hardly see at all.' I was so moved, I was at a loss for words to answer.

It was 11 years since I first met O'Casey.[1] He was an openhearted man and we soon struck rapport; he became a willing subject and in due course I was referred to as 'that photographer with the genial Albanian face.'

The quarry I stalked with my camera was a man of contrast: solicitous or stubborn by turn, as charmingly perverse as a gamin, and utterly responsive to a show of affection. Lost in thought, he looked as grave as a Church of England prelate at prayer. He could act a magnificent Paycock, or Joxer, or Juno if he must, and he would sing a hearty song for the asking. He would sit glued to the radio for hours listening to the cricket matches. Outdoors he always wore a ten-gallon hat two sizes too large, which had seen better days. He spent time in the garden which he had planted with lots of string beans, and, standing among the winding vines, could almost be mistaken for a scarecrow.

He openly professed to be a Communist, but this fiercely independent spirit neither talked nor acted like one. He had no illusions what his fate would be had he lived in Russia. 'I should be put

---

* *Life* (Chicago), 57 (9 October, 1964), pp. 92–3. International Edition, 37 (2 November, 1964), p. 53.

† Photographer on the staff of *Life* magazine. Some of his photographs of O'Casey are included in Eileen O'Casey's memoir, *Sean*. He was also responsible for the camera-work for the MGM film *Young Cassidy* (1965).

1. Mili had photographed O'Casey at his home in Totnes for the pictorial feature, 'The World of Sean O'Casey', *Life*, 23 August, 1954, which, later, formed the impetus for the making of the film *Young Cassidy*.

against the wall and shot,' he said. It was much later during my stay with him that I learned what, in a pragmatic way, he meant by Communism. Speaking about a youth who had come to him to seek advice, he told me, 'The lad is troubled. He cannot make up his mind whether or not to become a Communist. I asked him what he wanted to do for a living. When he answered, "A doctor," I told him "Be you the best practising doctor that ever lived—not only for those who can afford you, but also for the poor, for thse wh cannot afford you —and you'll be the best practising Communist that ever lived." ' This necessity to do good for others was characteristic of this poet of the poor who in his youth did unwelcome chores around union halls gratuitously and, though a Protestant, would spare no efforts to raise funds to buy milk for St Larry O'Toole's parish children by staging theatrical performances.

I was shocked to learn that for all his extraordinary gift for writing, after a lifetime of prodigious effort, O'Casey's yearly income was substantially less than $3,000. He recalled how it was his wife Eileen who gently but firmly had steered him away from accepting 'rich' movie offers which might compromise his independence. He chuckled. It would have made him unbearably unhappy, too hard to live with, she had said. By and large, the O'Caseys had adjusted their needs to their income and lived quite happily. There was the time we were going to dine out, and Niall, the younger son, peeling off his back the only heavy sweater in the house, made his father wear it for protection against the evening chill and stayed home himself when he had planned to go out. Niall's tragic death at barely twenty-one from leukaemia was a terrible blow. It almost broke O'Casey.[2] But he kept himself busy, writing steadily 'so as not to think too much of what Niall was, and what he hoped to be.'[3]

*   *   *

My visit now was made during a break I had in the filming of *Young Cassidy*, which is based on O'Casey's own account of his Dublin days. Once I was greeted and inside his Torquay flat, the visit was festive and, for a while, quite feverish. There was much to remember, much to relish. The past led to the present and the making of the film. Was it going well? And how was it in Dublin? I went

2. See also *Sean*, by Eileen O'Casey, pp. 258-9.
3. O'Casey's own moving account, 'Under a Greenwood Tree He Died', is included in *Under a Colored Cap*, pp. 100-33.

into a detailed description of the city today. The chaste roofs of Dublin's Georgian tenements were now literally transformed into vast forests of television antennas, tall and powerful enough to receive London. Ironically enough, in order to keep the illusion of Dublin of the twenties, it was costing the *Young Cassidy* company $50,000 to take down the antennas in the various locations where they planned to shoot.

O'Casey said in his amused, forbearing tone of voice, 'And have you come to take more pictures?' I began shooting him, standing by the mantelpiece below an early portrait of him by his good friend Augustus John, exactly as I had done eleven years ago. . . . He sat down on the couch to rest in the swiftly dying light.

Next morning I found him, once again on the couch in the living room, decked out in a red, monk-like robe which his daughter Shivaun had made. And there was that look which seemed to reflect in his face the wit and the wisdom, and all that is good in life. I told him how, on my various travels, when lonely, I would often recall one of his poems, 'The Dreamer's Song' from *Within the Gates*, to cheer me up.

> Her legs are as pliant and slim
> As fresh, golden branches of willow;
> I see lustre of love on each limb,
> looking down from the heights of a pillow! . . .

He saw through my stratagem but gallantly took the bait and in an uneven and often rasping voice started singing. Carried away with feeling, he looked young, much stronger, but soon his voice broke and he started to run out of breath. I was relieved when Eileen came in and, with a loving kiss, ushered Sean to his pre-lunch nap. Later we sat down at the table. Eileen had found my twenty-year-old, faded, blue-black corduroy hat. She thought it would look well on Breon, the elder son, but would Sean please try it on for size? He did and it caused great merriment. Sean ate sparingly, one soft-boiled egg, and mostly drank tea. It seemed he was anxious to light his trusty old pipe, and then, as if to put off making up his mind, he rose gently and bade me a heartfelt adieu. Then off he went to take his siesta.

Over those eleven years, my encounters with him were brief. But they were electric. And it was how I came to know—which is to say to love—Sean O'Casey.

Towards the End*

DAVID KRAUSE †

'Tell them I'm only talking to God now,' Sean said, prophetically as it turned out, for that was barely thirteen days before he died. I had answered the phone and called to him to say it was a reporter from London asking for permission to come down to Torquay to interview him, and he had sung out his reply in mock-solemnity, to the world and all its reporters: he was too busy talking to God. He hadn't sounded like a man who was dying, yet if he himself had sensed the end was near he had chosen to hide his secret in a characteristic jest about a serious thing, his shriving time. We will never know the nature of that holy and probably merry dialogue between God and O'Casey, but there can be little doubt that when it was over, Sean was cleared and ready to pass on to the heaven in which he often said he did not believe. 'I'm an atheist, thank God,' he liked to say, taking pleasure and comfort in this paradoxical phrase of Shaw's. Heretical humanist though he was, in his beginning and in his ending O'Casey was God's man and he was his own man. Since he believed that 'the best way to fit oneself for the next world was to fit oneself for this world', he must have died as he had lived, in a state of grace.

Few men had made themselves more fit for life in this world. If we were to venture a guess, perhaps that was what he was talking about with God, life not death. 'I will show you hope in a handful of life,' he once said to me when we were discussing T. S. Eliot's *The Waste Land*. He was too full of life to brood about fear and dust. For his wife and children, for his friends, there was no thought of his dying that year, or indeed at any time. He had survived so

* *Massachusetts Review* (Amherst), 6, no. 2 (Winter–Spring, 1965), pp. 233–51, originally entitled, 'Sean O'Casey: 1880–1964'. Reprinted in Robin Skelton and David R. Clark (eds.) *Irish Renaissance* (Dublin: Dolmen Press, 1965); also in Sean McCann (ed.) *The World of Sean O'Casey*, pp. 137–57, as 'Towards the End'.

† Associate Professor in English at Brown University, Rhode Island. Author of *Sean O'Casey: The Man and His Work* (London: MacGibbon and Kee; New York: Macmillan, 1960) and numerous articles on the playwright's work. At present engaged in editing O'Casey's Collected Letters.

many pains and ordeals throughout his eighty-four years, earning
his grace in the traditional way, through suffering, that those of us
who loved him seemed to sense some intimations of eternal life in
him, and we were somehow unable to conceive of the world without
Sean in it. It was only after he had suffered his fatal heart attack on
18 September [1] that we sought to temper our sorrow with amazement: 'The wonder is, he hath endur'd so long.'

He still seemed far from the end of his endurance when I met him
for that last time on a bright week-end early in September. I had
already seen him twice before for several weeks during the summer
in June and July, and now I had stopped at Torquay again on my
way back from Dublin for the usual farewell visit before setting out
on my homeward journey. He moved about more carefully now
than he had earlier in the summer, for he was still recovering from
an attack of his recurring bronchitis and other respiratory complica-
tions that had affected his heart, an illness which had laid him low
in August and sent him, over his protests, to a nearby nursing home
for several days. Apparently this attack had been more serious than
anyone realised, but at the time we did not think it was cause for
alarm, for he had come through greater dangers in the past. The
worst was in 1956 when he had fought his way back from two major
operations, kidney and prostate, only to have his heart broken at the
end of the year when his twenty-one-year-old son Niall died suddenly
of leukæmia. He was a long time recovering from that shock.

Sean had minimised his August illness, refusing to behave like an
invalid. In fact, shortly after we met in September and had settled
ourselves comfortably in his room, as if to convince me and himself
that he was not about to perform his swan song, he leaped nimbly
out of his chair and enacted an energetic mime-dance, pacing around
the room in an exaggerated strut, raising himself on tip-toe with each
swinging stride and flapping his arms so that he looked like a comical
old bird trying to fly and not quite making it. 'It keeps me from
forgetting that human beings are gay and funny fellas,' he said with a
broad grin as he sat down, rearranging the brightly-coloured beanie
on the back of his head. 'And besides, it's good for the circulation.' I
had begun by asking about his recent illness and he had demonstrated
his reply, which was good for our mutual circulation. No, I thought,
that dancing Sean was not a dying man.

But there was another shadow over his life now, in his mind

1. 1964.

more terrible than death, the increasing threat of total blindness. He had lived with this danger all his life, for his eyes had troubled him since childhood when he developed an ulcerated cornea in his left eye, which thereafter remained dim and filmy, and this placed a heavy strain on his already weakened 'good' eye, which periodically became ulcerated. Every day of his life he had to sponge his eyes with water as hot as he could bear it in order to wash away the sup-purating fluid that burned his eye-sockets and temporarily blotted out his vision. Over the many years that I had visited him, since 1954, I can hardly remember a day when he did not have to pause several times, in the afternoon and evening, remove his thick-lens glasses, press his thumb and fore-finger over his closed and burning eyes, and then go to the sink in his room for the ritualistic eye-washing.

As if this affliction were not enough, some of the hairs on his lower eyelids grew irregularly, pointing inward so that they jabbed at his eyeballs like needles, and this meant that often his wife or one of the children had to pull them out with a pair of tweezers. Sometimes the hairs were difficult to see, let alone pull, and meanwhile he would have to endure the pin-pricking pain, which grew worse with each flick of his eyelid. I was initiated into this ritual myself during my July visit, for when his wife Eileen, who said she had plucked thousands of such hairs from his eyelids throughout their marriage, had trouble locating a seemingly invisible hair that was torturing him, I was urged to have a go at it. As I held his magnificent bony head up to the light and probed with the tweezers, I trembled lest I should tear away some of his skin with the stubborn hair. Fortunately I was able to nip the hair and pull it out cleanly. It couldn't have been more than a 32nd of an inch in length, and he thanked me for delivering from him 'that bloody whoreson of a hair'.

He had been relieved of his pain by a stabbing 32nd of an inch, but nothing, neither science nor God, could save his fading eye-sight, which was apparently suspended now by little more than a hair's breadth. 'There is no pain he would not more willingly endure than blindness,' his wife had said to me in an aside in the kitchen. He did not talk much about it, but it was obviously troubling him and was especially apparent in the way he strained and squinted at any written material, with the page of a letter or book held so close to his right eye that it pressed against his nose. So I discussed the matter with his wife when we were alone after I first arrived in

June. Sean rested in bed for several hours every afternoon from around 2.30 to 4.30, a habit he had developed more to relieve his eyes than to sleep. He would slip a knotted handkerchief over his eyes and doze, or just lie there thinking; maybe he rehearsed some lines for a new play, or did what he called talking with God. While he rested, Eileen and I went for a stroll and had our talk. We walked from the crest of St Marychurch, the hilly suburb of Torquay where they lived, down the winding streets to the red cliffs of Babbacombe, overlooking a vast panorama of azure sea and sky. It was a familiar walk which Sean had taken with us in previous and better years, he with a cloth cap tipped low over his forehead to protect his eyes from the dazzling light and high wind, an ashplant swinging in one hand, the other linked snugly in Eileen's. Although he was about twenty-five years older than her, anyone who saw them would have known immediately that they were deeply in love with each other.

Eileen O'Casey is a strikingly handsome woman of auburn beauty and fine proportions, an open-faced woman with a gentle manner and a quick smile; and as if nature had not been generous enough to her, she also had the great good fortune to have lived with Sean O'Casey for thirty-seven years. Like her husband she was born and raised in Ireland, but later went to England to pursue a career in the theatre. She became an actress in London, met Sean when she played the role of Nora Clitheroe in his *Plough and the Stars*, and soon afterwards married him, in 1927. Since she was a Roman Catholic, they were married in church by a priest and their three children were properly baptised. But she no longer practises her faith, she practises Sean's faith.

We had moved away from the windy tor and settled under a tree on a grassy slope that led down to the sea-front. Then she began to talk about Sean's eyes. 'All the doctors say that in medical terms he should be blind now, and yet he can still see, just barely, because he wants to see, he needs to see in order to go on with his life and work. He couldn't bear to become a burden to us. So he sees through an act of will, an act of faith, and that's the way he has done everything all his life.' He could never be indifferent about anything, she said, no matter how minor it might be. He couldn't stand carelessness or untidiness, and always took great pains to be neat and clean in his personal habits. It worried him that he might one day become weak and helpless. He always had time for laughter and merriment, she said, but he had to keep his life and his mind in order.

They had gone up to London for several days early in the year to see a specialist when his already dim sight had suddenly begun to deteriorate at an alarming rate. After extensive examinations and X-rays, the specialist and his consultants had concluded that his left eye was stone blind, and there was little more than a faint flicker remaining in the right eye, so that while he might make out some vague shapes, he couldn't really see any more. His eyes were simply worn out. 'It was a terrible shock,' she continued. 'And yet, when we returned home he went back to his regular routine, writing letters every day, working on his new book of essays, and making plans for a new play. He couldn't read and I helped him with that, as I had in the past, though he did manage somehow to make out an odd word here and there. The doctors said he was blind, but he went on scribbling notes and touch-typing day after day. And on top of that came the bad news that we might have to move, and the mere thought of it terrified me. He would never survive that.'

Their landlord had died and there was a strong chance that the house would be sold, which meant they would probably have to vacate their flat. They rented the second floor of an old villa that had been divided into three separate dwellings, located on the highest spot in St Marychurch, with green rolling valleys below them spreading out to the sea, which was visible on clear days. In good weather Sean sat in the sun on their small stone porch, wearing his broad-brimmed felt hat, or he went down to wander among the flowers and the birds in their garden—'fifteen steps and then six steps, mind them carefully', as he often cautioned me. They were stony and steep.

'He knows the exact distance of everything in the house,' Eileen continued, 'and when people see him moving about so freely and confidently they don't realise that like a blind person he does it all by memory and instinct. If we have to move to a new place he'll become confused and go crashing into furniture and walls and break an arm or leg, and he'll probably be demoralised or dead in a week. He'll be all right if we can stay here.' That was in June. The threat of having to move hung over them all summer. But in the end, in September, it was not his eyes but his heart that failed him. As his good friend Brooks Atkinson wrote in a moving tribute, 'In eighty-four years of unselfish living it was the first time that his heart had failed him.' [2]

2. *New York Times*, 22 September, 1964, p. 36.

There was no sign of failure in him when we met early in September. He was tired from the boredom of his convalescence, but his mind was fully alert and his humour was characteristically sly.

'What does God say when you talk to Him?' I had asked after we had dispensed with the London reporter.

'He tells me the world is full of fools but he loves them anyway.'

'And what about you, do you love them anyway?'

'I only have trouble loving them when their folly grows out of stupidity instead of honest ignorance. Then I'm more inclined to hate them, or to hate the things that make them stupid. I love everyone and everything that's alive. I'm only indifferent to the dead. And now, for the love o' God, don't be asking so many foolish questions and let's get on with our work.'

'Our work' was the problem of trying to clear up countless questions and references in his letters, which I was collecting and editing. He had exchanged letters with some of the major literary figures of his time, but he also corresponded with hundreds of unknown people from many countries, people who praised or criticised his works, asked him to explain or justify something he had written, carried on extended discussions about literature and life, politics and religion, told him their troubles, asked his advice, and even named their children after him. Throughout all the years that his plays were not being produced, these people became his intimate audience, and so the daily ceremony of writing and receiving letters kept him in constant touch with the world of ordinary people who apparently read and reacted to everything he wrote. He had written thousands of letters over the past fifty years, many of which I had been able to locate during a three-year search, and there were situations and controversies to straighten out, people and places to identify, and an involved network of events in his life to correlate. I had worked out a good deal of it, but a number of mysteries remained. Some of these matters taxed his memory, which was understandable, especially exact dates and time sequences, yet on many of them he seemed to possess an uncanny total recall. Often the point in question had happened forty or fifty years ago and, since I had been able to put together some of the pieces during my investigations in Dublin, I usually had enough details to know that his version was in all probability accurate, rounded out with shrewd and comic observations on why some people had spoken or acted as they did. He invariably told his stories in dialogue, giving what the others had said and what he had

said, acting out all the parts in a well-flavoured style, and he was an
excellent mimic. Listening to him one would have guessed that Sean
himself was the original of the 'fluthered' Irishmen that Barry Fitzgerald had created in his plays. He spoke in a rasping tenor voice,
drawing out the syllables of words with a consequential Dublin
brogue that still retained the lilting cadences heard on the northside
of the Liffey. He could smile like a Dublin charwoman and swear
like a Dublin docker.

But there was much more in him than the randy comedian. There
was a glint of steel in his bony face, power in his transfixed eyes,
courage in the bite of his jaw. There was a craggy grandeur in his
aquiline profile which sometimes invested him with the magisterial
dignity of a Renaissance Cardinal painted by El Greco, especially
when he complemented his perennial red beanie by wearing his
blood-red robe on chilly days. His small eyes burned fiercely behind
his thick glasses and he could lower his voice to a mighty whisper of
rage when he reacted to some injustice in the world.

But there was much more in him than the courageous patriarch.
By nature a shy and gentle man, he was uncommonly tender and
solicitous with people he trusted, a gallant charmer with women
and children, a sweet companion with friends. There was a gesture
of ceremonial fun in the assortment of gaily designed and coloured
beanies or skull-caps he always wore, some of them made by his
daughter, others sent to him from friends all over the world. He
smoked a pipe continuously, and he might drink an occasional glass
of wine with guests, but he was a whiskey teetotaller; for he remembered too well his early life in Ireland when the labourers were paid
in the pubs and often drank up their wages before they could bring
them home to their wives and children. He loved all kinds of music.
During his younger days in Dublin he had worn a saffron kilt and
played the bagpipes, and he fancied himself something of a singer.
At any moment he might burst into song with a lively ballad—perhaps one of his own, for he had written songs for all his plays—and
whatever it may have lost in his croaking voice it gained in his delicate feeling. He was a man of deep impulses, and he could be moved
so profoundly by the misfortune of a friend, or even a stranger, that
he became ill with grief. For many of his achievements, he had a
tendency to doubt the merit of his work: 'Tell me what you thought
was bad in it, not what was good,' he said to me on a number of
occasions after I had praised something he had written.

His moods were often mixed, and he could be an outraged comedian, a gentle genius, an insecure rebel. Perhaps he had lived too long in self-imposed exile from his native land, for his extended quarrel with Ireland was a lover's quarrel: he was impatient with his country's frailties but would leap to the defence if an outsider attacked them. He was capable of unwarranted extremes and could make rash judgements from reasonable assumptions; he could see slights where none were intended; he could be quick to anger and slow to forgive. Sometimes he rolled out his heavy weapons for minor skirmishes, and he could hurl rhetorical thunderbolts when he felt he had been unjustly used or abused.

When I mentioned some of these extremes to him he shook his head sadly, then rubbed his beanie so vigorously that wisps of silvery hair flared wildly around its edges: 'Put it down to my tactlessness,' he said, 'my inability to keep my big mouth shut, much to my sorrow and the sorrow of others. But what was the alternative?' He rubbed his beanie with another flourish and straightened his back. 'Tact? Polite submission, that's what tact really is, and it's something I never learned. Children are naturally tactless, but it's knocked out of them in school where they learn to be polite and submissive. I never had any formal education and maybe that's why I became the way I am.'

'Are you saying that formal education is a dangerous thing because it isn't dangerous enough?' I asked.

'I'm saying there should be a way of teaching young people without breaking their spirit and making them so damned submissive. When they learn right from wrong they shouldn't be afraid to say so if they see it around them, and they shouldn't be so refined that they're unable to do anything about it. The first thing a fella has to do if he wants to accomplish anything of value is to be tactless. The world is full of powerful people who want everyone else to bow down before them and be tactful, and if they're not running the schools they're running the churches. But formal religion is worse than formal education when it comes to filling people full of fear and submission. Did you ever see anyone as tactful as a bishop?

'But Christ wasn't very tactful, was He? Let's face up to it, He was a great public nuisance, always stirring things up, always telling people what they should and shouldn't do, and so few of them ever listening to Him and He had to shout it out again and again. Was He polite and submissive? Was he afraid to speak out? All for one and one for all, that's what He preached, and He was a great communist.'

'Christ, a communist?' I asked.

'Of course He was. Read Shaw's great Preface to *Androcles and the Lion*. I wonder do they teach that in the schools, or in the churches? Christianity was communist from the beginning, it had to be if all men were to hold all things in common and be their brothers' keepers. But you'd never know it from the way the clergy talk and act today, for they're all tactful capitalists now. Read what Christ said in the Bible: "Ask, and it shall be given you; seek and you shall find; knock, and it shall be opened unto you". The world needs more of them—Askers and Seekers and Knockers. Now take that word Knock, that's a fine word—Knock, Knock, Knock. There are many doors in the world that need a powerful Knock. Read what Shaw said about what Christ said and did. "Gentle Jesus meek and mild is a snivelling modern invention, with no warrant in the gospels", that's what Shaw said. We can't get around it, you see, Christ was a tactless communist, God help Him, so don't be so damned sceptical about it.'

'It's just this, Sean,' I said, 'every time I hear you talk about Christianity and communism, the Star of Bethlehem and the Red Star seem to become interchangeable, as they do in your play, *The Star Turns Red*. And I have a strong feeling that the Russians, to say nothing of the Christians, would be even more sceptical than I am.'

'Ah, what is the stars?' he said with mischievous smile. 'They're all in the one blue sky that shelters every mother's son, Christian and communist, beggar and thief.'

That was a typical response. Whenever he got around to telling me what communism was and why he was a communist, he often began as if he were determined to drive the moneychangers out of the temple and ended by becoming gentle and dreamy. It wasn't that he was trying to be evasive, for he was wholly dedicated and even visionary on this subject. He was essentially a yea-sayer and loved to introduce hallelujah quotations from the Psalms in his conversation. How often I have heard him emphasise a point with one of the following phrases: 'Make a joyful noise unto God. . . . Blow up the trumpet in the new moon. . . . O let the nations be glad and sing for joy. . . . O sing unto the Lord a new song. . . .' He was tired of the old songs and pietistic slogans. He felt that the political jargon and cold-war clichés of the West and East had obscured the basic goals of

mankind, and he could set forth goals in a disarming if over-
simplified manner when he said, 'Every man who puts his best effort
into his life and work, be he a doctor or a bricklayer, is a communist
whether he knows it or not, for he's helping to improve the common
good, making the world a better place for himself and his family
and his country, and all the countries of the world.' Thus, communism was his touchstone for the ideal society, and the fact that it
was a scare-word to many people only increased his impulse to use it,
tactlessly, as he would have said. It was his way of knocking on
doors.

He seldom mentioned Marx or Lenin when he spoke about communism, for he was more likely to quote from Christ and Shaw,
Shelley and Keats, Blake and Burns, Emerson and Whitman, Ruskin
and Morris. On one occasion he called my attention to a little known
passage in Keats's poem 'Isabella' in order to show me 'what communism was all about'. He asked me to take the book from his shelf
and read the stanzas aloud to him, and he joined me from memory
on the third stanza so that we must have sounded like a Greek
chorus:

> With her two brothers this fair lady dwelt,
>   Enriched from ancestral merchandise,
> And for them many a weary hand did swelt
>   In torched mines and noisy factories,
> And many once proud-quiver'd loins did melt
>   In blood from stinging whip;—with hollow eyes
> Many all day in dazzling river stood,
>   To take the rich-ored driftings of the flood.
>
> For them the Ceylon diver held his breath,
>   And went all naked to the hungry shark;
> For them his ears gush'd blood; for them in death
>   The seal on the cold ice with piteous bark
> Lay full of darts; for them alone did seethe
>   A thousand men in troubles wide and dark:
> Half-ignorant, they turn'd an easy wheel,
>   That set sharp racks at work, to pinch and peel.
>
> Why were they proud? Because their marble founts
>   Gush'd with more pride than do a wretch's tears?—
> Why were they proud? Because fair orange-mounts

Were of more soft ascent than lazar stairs?—
Why were they proud? Because red-lin'd accounts
Were richer than the songs of Grecian years?—
Why were they proud? again we ask aloud,
Why in the name of Glory were they proud?

He took great delight in repeating the questions in the final stanza, and many times thereafter, when we happened to be talking about the oppressors and the oppressed of the world, he would roar out the last two lines in a lusty chant:

Why were they proud? Again we ask aloud,
Why in the name of Glory were they proud?

So he would usually turn to literature or the Bible when he wanted to underscore the nature of his communism, which was more deeply rooted in ethical values than in a political system. And it is not surprising that these values should have developed out of the doctrines of Christianity, for what little formal education he had received as a boy was obtained in the Church of Ireland. He had to leave the church school, St Mary's, at an early age because of his weak eyes, which were covered with ointments and bandages for several hours of every day. He recorded some of this information in his autobiography,[3] but since he was vague about specific details I always tried to locate documented evidence during my visits to Dublin. On one occasion I found a copy of his Confirmation papers which indicated that he had been confirmed at Clontarf Church in 1898, at the age of eighteen, that he had received his First Communion on Easter Day of that same year at St Barnabas Church, and that he had been baptised in 1880 at St Mary's. For a long time he had been uncertain about the day and year of his birth, and a search through the files of the Registry Office, under his baptised name of John Casey, revealed the date as 30 March, 1880.

Two summers ago I brought back from Dublin a copy of another forgotten document out of his past to show him, this time the record of a prize he had won in Sunday School at the age of seven. It read as follows: 'Church of Ireland, United Dioceses of Dublin, Glendalough and Kildare. At a Diocesan Examination in Connexion with the Board held at St Mary's Schoolhouse on the (the day is blank) of 1887, II Class was awarded to John Casey of St Mary's Parish for

3. *I Knock at the Door.*

Proficiency in Holy Scripture and Church Formularies. Signed, Plunkett—Dublin.' (the Archbishop).

'Are you sure it was only a second class prize?' he asked when I read it to him.

'No doubt about it, it says second class.'

'Ah, well,' he said with a grin, 'that's not so bad for a half-blind little chiseller.' [4]

'Then you do remember your childhood proficiency in Holy Scripture?'

'I remember it as through a glass lightly. It must have been the year after my father died. He was a great reader of books, and that was unusual then, for he was the only person in the neighbourhood who actually had bookcases filled with them. I wasn't able to read at the age of seven, because of my eyes, but like all children I could repeat anything if I heard it several times. The Bible was the important book in our house, and full of fine stories and mysterious words for a curious kid to imitate. I liked the sound of the words long before I knew what they meant, and it gave me a feeling of power to spout them in the house and in front of the other kids. And don't forget, my sister Isabella was a teacher at St Mary's so she stuffed me full of the right things to say to make certain I didn't disgrace her and the family name. Then there was my dear Mother, who never missed a Sunday at church, and later there was the Reverend Edward Griffin of St Barnabas. I was a stubborn kid with a mind of my own, but I wouldn't have done anything to let them down.'

Only last summer I had located one of the Reverend Griffin's daughters. She had gone to England with her clergyman husband, but now they were living in retirement in Ireland. She gave me some of her recollections of Sean—'John not Sean, he was John Casey when we knew him'—as a young man of twenty-four at St Barnabas, the details of which I corroborated with him during my July visit. Sean, or John, and her father, the Rector, were as close as father and son in those days. At the particular time that she remembered, around 1904, prayer-meetings were often held on week-day evenings in the Church schoolhouse, and at the conclusion of the service the Rector would ask for a volunteer to lead the final prayer. 'It was then,' she said, 'after an awkward pause while father waited for the volunteers, that my sister and I—we were girls of eight and ten—would nudge each other and whisper, "It'll be John again, he'll jump up again,

4. More usually, *chiselur*: Gaelic expression for 'child'.

and oh, he'll go on and on as he always does." He sat behind us and
we were afraid to turn round and look, but soon we heard his voice
ringing out loud and clear, in that drawling, lilting way he had of
speaking. He didn't read from the prayer-book as the others did, he
just made up his prayer as he went along, using some biblical passages but mostly his own words about the glory of God. As I said, at
the time my sister and I joked about how he would go on and on
with it, but we were silly little girls then, and when I think of it all
now it comes back to me as something very moving and beautiful.
He would have made a great preacher.'

Maybe he did become something of a lyrical preacher, especially
in his later plays where he wrote humorously and heroically about
the joy of life, in the fantasy of an enchanted Cock or in the ecstasy
of a miracle on the banks of the Liffey. In the latter instance, in *Red
Roses for Me*, when his autobiographical hero, Ayamonn Breydon,
who attends a Church called St Burnupus and is a close friend of
the Rector, joins the people of Dublin in a transformation dance
and exhorts them to seek a new life, he may well have been making
up another of his lilting prayers : '*Friend, we would that you should
live a greater life; we will that all of us shall live a greater life. Our
sthrike is yours. A step ahead for us today; another one for you to-
morrow. We who have known, and know, the emptiness of life shall
know its fullness. All men and women quick with life are fain to
venture forward. The apple grows for you to eat. The violet grows
for you to wear. Young maiden, another world is in your womb. . . .
Our city's in th' grip o' God.*'

The Rector's daughter also remembered that John was interested
in other things besides prayer in those days, which explained why
he soon changed his name to Sean. 'He was full of the Gaelic language and told us proudly that no Irishman was a true Irishman
unless he could speak Irish. You see, on Sundays after church he
often accompanied my sister and me on the long walk from St
Barnabas to the Rectory, which was on Charles Street of Mountjoy
Square. First we would walk his mother home, around the corner
on Abercorn Road. We always called her Granny Casey. She was
a neat little woman, she wore a pretty bonnet, and she gave us sweets.
When we set out on our walk John was swinging a hurley stick,
which he hid outside the Church. It was an ancient Irish game, he
told us, and Irishmen should be proud to play it. After he left us at
the Rectory, he went on to Jones's Road to play with his friends.

Well, on those walks he would tell us stories about the Irish heroes, and sing songs in Irish. Once he taught us the chorus of 'Cruiskeen Lawn', the part that's in Irish, and do you know, I still remember those lines:

> *Gramachree, mavourneen, slanta gal avourneen,*
> *Gramachree ma Cruiskeen Lawn, Lawn, Lawn.*

'He sang the song and we joined in on the chorus. We must have been a strange sight as we marched along singing merrily, two little girls in our Sunday dresses and John waving out the rhythm with his hurley stick.'

'Like the pied piper of Dublin,' I said to him. 'You kept your faith in the Irish language through the years, but when did you lose your faith in the Church?'

'I never lost my faith, I found it, I found it when Jim Larkin came to Dublin a few years later and organised the unskilled labourers. I found it in Jim's great socialist motto: "An injury to one is the concern of all".'

'Socialist and Christian?'

'Socialist and Christian. They're both the one thing—communism —if only the people knew it. Jim knew it as well as he knew his penny-catechism, but the clergy condemned him for it during the 1913 strike, saying hell wasn't hot enough nor eternity long enough for the likes of him. Yet he was the Saviour of Dublin. He put his faith in the people and their need to live a better and fuller life. And that's where I put my faith.'

We must take him at his word and deed, for that is the faith to which he devoted his life as man and artist. He expressed it in his plays in comedy and tragedy, farce and fantasy. He expressed it in his autobiography and books of essays in narrative, argument and satire. He was a visionary humanist, a man of this worldly spirit. As an artist, the form as well as the substance of his plays is of such a magnitude that even in death he remains ahead of his time, for there is still no theatre able or daring enough to do justice to his pioneering achievements in dramatic technique, beginning with *The Silver Tassie*. He spent the last thirty-six years of his life exploring new forms, rejecting all the orthodoxies and conventions of the theatre, even his own.

He was writing about that form and faith right to the end. When I saw him a fortnight before he died, he was finishing a satirical essay called 'The Bald Primaqueera.'[5] The joke in the title is aimed at the theatre of the absurd and alludes to Ionesco's play *The Bald Prima Donna*, known in America as *The Bald Soprano*. Sean said he was fed up with what he called 'absurd plays by absurd playwrights who sing the same dreary song on the one weary note and then have the gall to make a bloody mystery of it'. He had in mind Ionesco and Pinter and their imitators. 'Not Beckett and Brecht,' he insisted, 'they have the leap of the life force in them, even when they're pessimistic, because they're poets as well as playwrights, and I like what they do with words. Ionesco and Pinter belong in the cinema where pictures and pauses are more important than words. And speaking of words, exciting words in the theatre, look at the plays of John Arden, the best of the young playwrights today. I have an aggressive admiration for his *Serjeant Musgrave's Dance*. But those absurd fellas, they'd put years on you. It's obvious they were never touched by the Holy Ghost.'

He was also fed up with what he called the 'primaqueera' element that he associated with the absurd ties in the theatre—'the bona fide homosexuals and pseudo-intellectuals who infest the theatre'. By coincidence, while we were checking through some letters, I came across several that he had written twenty years ago to a friend in the London theatre. At that time he had expressed similar views, and when the friend protested that Sean was prejudiced, he had replied: 'I shouldn't call dislike of "conceited amateurs, arrogant homosexuals, & impertinent dilettantes" a prejudice. I hate them—except when they're comic, like most of our Irish ones. We don't hate enough in England. The English don't know how. They think it a virtue. It isn't. It shows lack of life force.' To which he added 'amen' twenty years later.

But at eighty-four and approaching blindness he was not yet ready to say 'amen' to life. Somehow he managed to press on with his work, a new book of essays. Every day he sketched out some ideas or wrote letters, writing laboriously with a pen or tapping away at the typewriter, and his wife knew things were going well if she heard him humming tunes to himself. But since his failing sight prevented him from re-reading what he had written, he had to have his wife or a friend [6] read it back to him so that he could think about where he had been and where he was going, make various changes, and move on

5. *Blasts and Benedictions*, pp. 63–76.
6. Ronald Ayling, editor of *Blasts and Benedictions*.

again. The genial gardener[7] came by once a week and he helped out with the reading and writing, also doing some of the re-typing. It was a slow and frustrating process, one which would have defeated anyone except a man like Sean, who was as patient as he was stubborn. So he went on with his words, asking and seeking and knocking. He was disturbed because his eyes were so bad that he could no longer read books. He regretted that he couldn't re-read Joyce, Shaw, Yeats, and George Moore, though he still retained a remarkable memory of their works. Joyce he loved the most. 'He tells us everything in *Finnegans Wake*, that beautiful book of reality.[8] I don't know what a lot of it means, but he created such magical patterns of words that I feel them long before I understand them; and often I simply feel them without understanding them. Only a true poet can do that to us.'

When we were together in June, talking about religion, he suddenly pointed his palms under his chin and chanted, 'In the name of Annah the Allmaziful, the Everliving, the Bringer of Plurabilities, haloed be her eve, her singtime sung, her rill be run, unhemmed as it is uneven.' He and his wife often talked about *Ulysses* and *Dubliners*, especially their favourite story, 'The Dead'. Eileen read to him every day, he listened to talks and plays on the radio, and to the recordings of classics sent down by the Society for the Blind.

I had read to him on our final evening together. We had taken a short walk before tea, up to the wall of St Mary's Church—in previous times we had regularly gone the whole distance around the wall and come back through the peaceful churchyard—and later we settled comfortably in his room. 'Don't call it my study,' he corrected me, 'it's where I work.' There were signs of his work everywhere in the room. Crowded bookcases lined the walls and books overflowed on the floor; piles of books and magazines were scattered over the large round table, at one end of which was an old Underwood typewriter with a half-typed sheet of paper in it; beside the machine a green eye-shade was hung over a gooseneck lamp; on the window ledge were two boxes stuffed with incoming and outgoing letters; a red morocco folder on the bed was full of sheets of paper on which he had scrawled notes and random phrases. The electric fire glowed brightly, and there was a pungent smell of tobacco in the air. Sean

7. Geoffrey Dobbie.
8. '*It is an amazing book; and hardly to be understood in a year, much less than a day.*' (Letter from O'Casey to Joyce, dated 30 May, 1939.)

sat on the bed puffing at his pipe, his legs stretched out and crossed at the angles, a red and white Tashkent beanie on the back of his head.

'Are ye there, truepenny?' he called.

'I see you have the new edition of poetry by Austin Clarke and Patrick Kavanagh.'

I had been browsing through some of the books on the table.

'Eileen was reading them to me. Clarke's a better poet than any of us knew, a fine poet. Poor fella, he was overshadowed by Yeats. But Yeats's shadow fell over everyone.'

I read some of Clarke's poems aloud. Eileen had read 'Forget Me Not' to him, so I began with the title poem of 'Flight to Africa', which drew some hearty laughter from him. Then I read from the *Later Poems*—'Inscription for a Headstone', 'Three Poems about Children', 'The Blackbird of Derrycairn', and 'Night and Morning'.

'Read the "Headstone" once again,' he asked, 'the one about Larkin.'

> What Larkin bawled to hungry crowds
> Is murmured now in dining-hall
> And study. Faith bestirs itself
> Lest infidels in their impatience
> Leave it behind. Who could have guessed
> Batons were blessings in disguise;
> When every ambulance was filled
> With half-killed men and Sunday trampled
> Upon unrest? Such fears can harden
> Or soften heart, knowing too clearly
> His name endures on our holiest page,
> Scrawled in a rage by Dublin's poor.

He was deeply moved by this ironic poem, for he had lived through the 'Bloody Sunday'[9] that it celebrated; he had served under Larkin at the time as secretary of the Irish Citizen Army; and he saw himself as one of the 'infidels' of 1913. His voice thickened with a Dubliner's rage at the mention of those times and Jim Larkin, the man he had called the Irish Prometheus. Then we talked about Jim Plunkett, who had written a play about Larkin and was now writing a novel[10] about

9. 30 August, 1913, during the great industrial lock-out, when hundreds of workers were injured in riots with the authorities.

10. *Strumpet City* (London, 1969).

S.T.—6*

the events leading up to the 1913 strike. 'Are there any people over there besides Jim Plunkett who still care about Larkin's Dublin?' he asked. 'Really care in their Christian hearts?' He relit his pipe angrily and sent great clouds of smoke billowing through the room.

He was silent for a while, and I began to read some of Kavanagh's poems of which he seemed to like 'Kerr's Ass' and passages from 'The Great Hunger' the best. When I had finished reading the last lines of 'The Great Hunger',

> The hungry fiend
> Screams the apocalypse of clay
> In every corner of this land,

it was clear that he was still brooding about Larkin. 'There it is again, the hungry fiend, in Mucker or in Dublin, and it takes the rage of a poet to put it right. Larkin was the poet of the people. Why even Yeats, aristocrat though he was—in his own mind not in his class—spoke out for Larkin and the workers.'

So we came at last to Yeats, and the poems of Yeats. Contrary to what many people thought, Sean insisted, he did not feel bitter towards Yeats because of the Abbey Theatre's rejection of *The Silver Tassie*. 'I was bloody mad at him, not bitter. That was in 1928 when I had a wife and a kid on the way, so the rejection meant hard times for the O'Caseys. But it wasn't only that, I was ripping mad because he was wrong about my play. And I still think he was wrong. Maybe one day there'll be a real production of that play—it's still one of my favourites, and I can see the whole thing, in my mind, glowing on a stage—then we'll find out who was right about it. After the rejection there were people in Dublin who did feel bitter towards Yeats—they always had, mainly because they were jealous and afraid of him—and they tried to get me to join them and go against him. Well, I told them what they could do with their dirty game, they could stuff it where the monkey put the nut. Yeats was wrong about my play, but he made the Abbey a great theatre, he and Lady Gregory. After he died it went downhill. There was no one left to fight for it and protect it from the political and clerical yahoos who torment the artist in Ireland. They're the fellas I feel bitter about.'

Then he began to praise Yeats as a poet. He didn't think much of him as a playwright. 'His poems are more dramatic than his plays, and his plays are really poems.' I began to read Yeats's poems to him, some of the *Last Poems*, which he especially wanted to hear. I read

'The Circus Animals' Desertion', 'Parnell', and 'The Spur'. Then I mentioned that Liam Miller [11] had set some of the poems to traditional Irish airs and had them sung by a group of young ballad singers in one [12] of Dublin's pocket theatres during the previous summer. This interested him and I read several of them, 'The Three Bushes' and 'The Ghost of Roger Casement'. He enjoyed them and said they had a word-music of their own which revealed another side of Yeats, his close touch with the people, from whom he usually remained aloof. 'That was part of his greatness,' Sean said, 'he hated the Irish crowd but he loved the Irish people.'

We closed out the evening with 'Under Ben Bulben', and Sean quoted the well-known fifth section from memory:

> Irish poets, learn your trade,
> Sing whatever is well made,
> Scorn the sort now growing up
> All out of shape from toe to top,
> Their unremembering hearts and heads
> Base-born products of base beds.
> Sing the peasantry, and then
> Hard-riding country gentlemen,
> The holiness of monks, and after
> Porter-drinkers' randy laughter;
> Sing the lords and ladies gay
> That were beaten into the clay
> Through seven heroic centuries;
> Cast your mind on other days
> That we in coming days may be
> Still the indomitable Irishry.

'Good poetry', he said, 'but bad advice for Irish poets. Is it the Ireland of aristocratic parasites and enslaved peasants he's asking us to go back to? The Ireland of plaster saints and hedge [13] scholars? The Ireland of the Big House and the little people? The Ireland of purple dust? Not bloody likely we'll go back to those corpses. But it's still a damn fine poem. And so like Yeats, to make good poetry of bad opinions. I wonder why he wasn't up to saying the same thing

11. Director of the Dolmen Press.

12. The Lantern Theatre, Dublin, where dramatisations of some of O'Casey's autobiographies have been staged.

13. Who taught in the absence of official teachers when the penal laws were in operation.

about *The Tassie*, that I might be able to write a good play out of what he thought were bad opinions? Ah, that's a head without a tail.'

Yeats had tried to make some amends for his rejection of *The Silver Tassie* when, in 1935, he finally had the play performed at the Abbey Theatre, in spite of virulent opposition. Thus, one of Yeats's last of many famous fights at the Abbey was for O'Casey; and when the two men met in Dublin for what turned out to be a final reunion in September of 1935—it was O'Casey's last visit to Ireland, and Yeats died four years later—they settled their differences as men, though they remained in different worlds as artists, but both of them symbolic of 'the indomitable Irishry' in their different ways.

Eileen had come in with a pot of tea for the road, for it was late and soon I would be leaving for America. When I finally stood up to go, Sean said, 'My favourite lines of Yeats are not from the last poems but from his first play, *The Countess Cathleen*. Do you remember what Oona says at the end, after the Countess has given up her soul to save Ireland?' And he intoned softly:

> Tell them who walk upon the floor of peace
> That I would die and go to her I love;
> The years like great black oxen tread the world,
> And God the Herdsman goads them on behind,
> And I am broken by their passing feet.

We walked out to the porch and he embraced me in a tender bear-hug.

'We've heard the chimes at midnight,' he said.

'Bless you, Sean.'

'And you, too. Give my love to America.'

'See you next summer.'

'Right-o,' he smiled, 'next summer, and all the summers that warm the green world.'

It was a clear night and the sky over St Marychurch was ablaze with stars. What are the stars? I don't know, but I knew they were all up there, 'all of them in the one blue sky that shelters every mother's son.' As I reached the end of the garden, I turned for one last look and caught a glimpse of him through the trees, standing at the top of the steps. He was still there in the gentle night, gazing at the stars.

I feel now as I felt then, that he would always be there, as long as the summers warmed the green world.

Last Thoughts from O'Casey*

'MANDRAKE' †

'First play ¹ I sent to the Abbey got a rejection slip from W. B. Yeats: "Not far from being a good play."

'I was writing plays—or tryin' to—on bits of old paper my friends picked up off the floor in the places they worked. Couldn't afford a bottle of ink, so I boiled old stubs of indelible pencil to make my own ink.'

His fourth attempt, the play *On the Run*—changed to *Shadow of a Gunman*—together with *Juno and the Paycock* saved the Abbey from literal bankruptcy. '*Gunman* grossed £90 at the box office. I got £4. I still had to go tearing up the roads with a pick and shovel.

'I'd changed my name to Sean O'Cathasaigh but now that I was having plays put on I changed it to O'Casey and kept the Sean.'

The full round beauty of Dublin's accent was still O'Casey's that day—he sounded his 't', like Joxer and Captain Boyle, as 'th'.

'In *Juno and the Paycock* there was a "Captain" Boyle and that was his real name. Would he have been insulted? He'd never even heard of the play but if he'd seen it he'd have been *proud* and delighted. Because all the people from the Dublin streets I wrote about liked me. Because I was one of them, in all me sinews and to the last breath in me body.

'I'm still writing, you know. Only me eyes . . . I can hardly see now. Last of it'll be I won't be able to see at all. I'll dictate instead. . . .

'This Filthy Theatre argument. Ph-auugh! I'm thinking of writing a new play myself.' The wide, humorous Irish mouth twitched, trying to keep the smile in. 'I'll be calling it *The Bald Primaqueera*.² You have to keep up with the times, you know. . . .

'The Theatre of Pessimism they call it? What did the feller say? "The world is an oyster with nothing in it."

* A shortened form of the article, 'Sunday Morning with "Mandrake": Last Thoughts from O'Casey', which appeared in the *Sunday Telegraph* (London), 20 September, 1964, p. 13.
  † The reporter who interviewed O'Casey on this occasion was John Summers, who also took one of the last photographs of the playwright.

1. *The Frost in the Flower.*
2. The title, in fact, of his last article: *Blasts and Benedictions*, pp. 63–76.

'But that's not pessimism.' Sean O'Casey's hand slapped his knee-cap. 'That's poet-thry!'

The Devon sea haze and the warm salt air blew gently through the open window, at sunset.

This was the O'Casey who was once quoted as saying that Ireland 'is my true and only love'.

True still?

Sean O'Casey raised his head. A look towards the sea. Then his head nodded once.

And once again.

Sean O'Casey, Saint and Devil*

GERARD FAY †

Sean O'Casey used to visit my mother and father from time to time in Dublin and they both said to him from different points of view that he ought to be more careful about using politics in his plays. My father's view was that the putting on the stage of such recent and bloodstained events was outside the scope of the 'art theatre' which he still conceived the Abbey to be. My mother was thinking more of his extreme left-wing views which coalesced in the end into Communism and cut him off to some extent from the three countries where he should most have flourished—Ireland, the United States and Britain.

He was for years a member of the board of management of the *Daily Worker* and he left only because the board of the People's Press Printing Society was reconstituted for legal reasons. He sent a highly congratulatory message for the 10,000th issue. Even his communism-anarchism or whatever it really was would hardly have fitted into the pattern of any monolithic state. What made even more difficult for him—for his plays, especially the early Dublin tenement

* *Guardian* (London), 21 September, 1964, p. 5.

† Journalist and author, who died in 1968, aged 54. London editor of the *Guardian*, and dramatic critic of the *Manchester Guardian* for several years. His father was Frank Fay and his uncle, W. G. Fay—both of whom evolved the Abbey Theatre's own acting style. Gerard Fay is the author of *The Abbey Theatre: Cradle of Genius* (London, 1958) and other works.

tragi-comedies (sometimes the ones he called tragedies were described as comedies by critics) continued to be produced widely—was what seemed to be a quarrelsome nature making him always the centre of controversy.

Well, he certainly liked a fight but was not by any means the acidulous sort of man who seemed to be shown by the way he bit the pens that praised him. He was certainly right as an artist to seek a way of breaking a way through his self-built wall of tenement drama.

He made a generalisation once which I am surprised has never been the subject of a doctorate thesis at an American university that on the whole the prophets of the Irish theatre (by which he meant the dramatists) were Protestants, the priests (he meant the actors and actresses) were on the whole Roman Catholics.

Like some other writers who can pour passion into every paragraph, and prejudice too, he was as gentle, compassionate, generous and loving a man as there could be. The same applied to a very different sort of Irish dramatist, Brendan Behan. 'Saintly' was the word for them, though they sometimes seemed to behave in a diabolical way.

When producers, especially abroad, have ceased to be hypnotised by *Juno*, *The Shadow*, *The Plough*, there are many other plays which will have to be looked at again for they contain much of the very best O'Casey wrote. A director of genius might, for instance, find a way of making all of *The Bishop's Bonfire* stand up to the first act, and *Red Roses for Me* and *Purple Dust* have much in them which could somehow be extracted.

But of course even if his plays faded from the scene for a while his multi-volume *Autobiography*, especially the earlier parts, will stand as a work of genius in English prose. I had a lively correspondence with him (lost, now, alas!) when he accused me of taking the side of the Church by gently chiding him for spending too much space on an alleged injustice to an Irish priest: I had said something to the effect that it wasn't very interesting to the general reader and wasn't his business particularly.

We sorted out the point about which side I was on but his crushing answer was 'Injustice anywhere in the world is my business, yes even including the Soviet Union.'

Another time he wrote, and I quote from memory, 'People get it all wrong about why my own countrymen dislike me and some hate me. It has to do with Irish politics, with world politics, but as often as not with religion. Some of them dare to write a bit of milk and water criticism of their own church now and then, but they won't have it from a black Prod.

'I quarrelled with the Citizen Army because I thought they ought to be training for guerrilla fighting, which has beaten great armies before now. They wanted fine uniforms and to march through the streets in them with bands and banners. I left the Army and they sneer at me that I make money out of describing fighting I never took part in; but I had as narrow escapes as many another Dubliner and nearly got shot out of hand before I was arrested on suspicion and kept in safety by the British Army.'

His own wars were never guerrilla ones but fought out in the open in set battles with battalions of sharp and searing words. One of the biggest ended in what he thought a victory—he forbade the production of his plays on any professional stage in his own country. They have been produced since then and will, no doubt, again.

I can see not very far into the future when Dublin will proudly present an O'Casey Festival and great pompous speeches will be made. O'Casey must have suspected this too for he told a friend only a few years ago—'they'll get me in the end. *They'll make me part of Ireland's Litherary Glory, God help me!*'

The Final Curtain*

BROOKS ATKINSON †

Perhaps it can be put this way: I knew that like all men Sean O'Casey must die some day. But it never occurred to me that he would. In the thirty years during which I knew him, he surmounted so many disasters that I was forgetting a basic fact of life.

He did not surmount a heart attack on Friday, 18 September, 1964, in a Torquay nursing home, where he had been a patient before. The Irishman who wrote the most glorious English of his time has

* *New York Times*, 22 September, 1964, p. 36, originally entitled 'In 84 Years of Unselfish Life, O'Casey Had His Heart Fail Him Only Once'.
† See note on p. 131.

dropped his pen. This column is in honour of the personal side of O'Casey—a god of wrath in his public postures but a kindly man with a modest view of himself in private life.

Both the public and the private personalities were authentic. An enemy of everything that corrodes the spirit, he was a belligerent writer. He could be outrageously quarrelsome in print. But at home he was simple, frank, warm, and talkative and very civil in the pursuit of an argument. The public fire became a private glow.

*   *   *

When I first met him in New York, when *Within the Gates* was produced, he was a sharp-faced, thin, animated Irishman with thick glasses to compensate for weak eyes. When I last visited him in December, 1962, in his cheerful flat on the second floor of a re-modelled house on a hill in Devon, he was still sharp-faced and thin. The lenses in his spectacles were still thick, but they could no longer compensate for eyes that had almost lost their vision.

'Joyous' may not be too radiant a word to describe his inner spirit in his last years. He was an optimist about the future of mankind. Despite the many hardships of his life (he once remarked that he regarded himself as a failure) he always enjoyed the experience of being alive: *'Tired, but joyous, praising God for His brightness and the will towards joy in the breasts of men'*—to quote a line he once wrote about himself as a tenement boy in Dublin. Although O'Casey aged, he never changed.

*   *   *

Since he had had little formal education and did not pretend to be a scholar, I was always amazed by the range of his knowledge. He seemed to know and relish just about everything in literature, including the Greek and Latin classics. Like most Irishmen, he was steeped in Irish history. He could wrangle about things that had happened in Ireland a thousand years ago as if they had just appeared in the newspapers. He knew English and American history in depth. He loved classical music and all kinds of paintings.

A man who enjoyed being alive in a sentient world, he was observant and knowledgeable about nature. Acknowledging a National Wildlife Federation stamp of the ivory-billed woodpecker, he replied last month: 'We have none of that variety here; but we have three others—the larger and lesser spotted, and the big green bird, a vivid green with a magnificent crimson-crested head. Once a month or so, one of these appears in our garden, hammering away at the trunks of the trees, a hammering that tells me my bird-friend or bird-brother is with us again.'

When he heard that I had visited the redwoods of California, he recalled that Dr Douglas Hyde, first president of the Gaelic League, had found the redwoods 'terrifying'. He went on to argue that the cypresses in his garden (*Cupressus macrocarpa*) are 'brothers minor' to the great trees of California. Like many people who lose their sight, he had vivid visual memories. One letter he wrote two years ago was a beautifully composed essay about some swallows he had seen in Dublin when he was a labourer in a construction gang.

*   *   *

How he found time to write so many letters to so many people was always a mystery because none of the letters were tossed off without style. In late years, when his sight was dim, a friend [1] typed them for him and his wife, Eileen O'Casey, helped him with everything.

No portrait of Sean would be complete without an expression of admiration for the main talents as well as the devotion of this energetic, good-humoured woman. Last March he itemised her household activities as follows: 'Eileen is snatching a little time to read the letters coming to me and a snatch of words from a book now and then, shopping and cooking, dealing with problems that at times disturb Shivaun [the O'Casey daughter] today and Breon [the son] and his family tomorrow, and keeping an eye out to save me from bumping into things, or tripping over them so that I don't end my life with a bang.'

He didn't end his life with a bang. His heart stopped beating. In 84 years of unselfish living it was the first time his heart had failed him.

1. Ronald Ayling.

Appendix A

O'Casey: For All his Curses, a Yea-Sayer*

HAROLD CLURMAN †

Listening to Sean O'Casey reading from various sections of his autobiography *Mirror in My House* [1] (Caedmon TC 1198) I became more aware than ever that his prose is music. Because of his advanced age at the time of the recording, O'Casey's voice is shaky and a bit thin. He probably never had Joyce's smooth, rich tenor. (Composers are not always the best instrumental interpreters or conductors of their compositions.) Yet one would miss something specially poignant if one never heard O'Casey reading, for there is in it an 'added' melody which his Hibernian rhetoric alone does not convey.

Even the slight monotony of the depressed sound which issues from a recital of a visit to the grocer's with his mother in *I Knock at the Door*—the book's first volume—lends it a sweet melancholy altogether fitting to the old man's recollection of his sad, faraway boyhood. The accent in which 'flattering' becomes '*flathering*', 'turnips' '*tornips*', 'biting' '*boiting*', 'butcher' '*boothcher*' is an odd orchestration which gives extra savour to the remembered scene.

All of O'Casey—in many respects the best of him—is to be found in the pages of these memoirs. When his speech can no longer contain the lyricism within him he sings his own or other poets' lines in a manner which one can without sentimentality call heartbreaking. It is a natural, almost demanded, heightening of tone corresponding to the speaker's feeling.

In the chapter entitled 'Life is More Than Meat', a beggar's song accompanies his mother's purchases of food: 'Hard times, hard times, come again no more.' And the words set the key to the entire

* *New York Times*, 23 November, 1969, p. 8.
 † American theatre director, manager and critic. Has written widely on the theatre, and has published *Lies Like Truth* (1958), a volume of drama criticism.

 1. American generic title for the six books of autobiography, 2 vols (New York: Macmillan Co., 1956).

passage. What is truly wonderful is that these sorrowful pages which picture the penury of Sean's boyhood, finish with Mrs Casside's tender and lofty scolding: he had stolen a mite of sugar, tea and jam at the store. 'Never do that again, Johnny. Remember what you've been taught: Take no thought for your life, what ye shall eat; nor yet for your body, what ye shall put on; for the life is more than meat, an' the body than raiment. . . .'

*   *   *

There is anger and a laughing bitterness in O'Casey where the mournfulness and lament come to an end. In his diatribe against the atom bomb (which he pronounces 'atom bumb'), all the elements of O'Casey's nature are conjoined: his indignation, humour, and great heart. 'Zap! There goes a great city! Send them up to heaven hot. . . . We have the atom bomb. Twinkle, twinkle mighty bomb, bring us safe to kingdom come; when you come with clouds ascending, doing harm that needs no mending; from the palace, hall, and slum bring us safe to kingdom come. . . . [Generals] love guns as kids love candies. They call upon people to get ready for war as if they were calling upon them to get ready for a walk. "The sight gladdens my old eyes," a general is alleged to have said, when he saw a heap of Korean dead. . . . The price we pay for a heap of Korean dead is a heap of our own dead; put out an eye, and lose one ourselves; a loss for a loss; I'm dead, you're dead, he's dead, we're all dead. . . . The military mind is indeed a menace.'

When O'Casey was sailing to the U.S. for the first time in 1934, 'the poorest cabin-passenger that had ever set foot on a White Star liner,' he looked towards the Statue of Liberty (which he could not see) calling it 'America's Lady of the Lamp'. He remembered its well-known inscription, 'Give me your tired, your poor . . . .'

'Little sparkle in the words now,' he comments. But he loved America. Bound for New York, he apostrophises the 'Manhattan of Walt Whitman'. Old Walt was surely one of his spiritual and literary forebears. 'Oh, Walt Whitman,' O'Casey exclaims, 'saintly sinner, sing for us—one of the world's good wishes is the one that wishes you here today, to sing Shake Hands to the world's people.' He speaks, too, of Whitman's 'embracing message'.

That message is also O'Casey's. What I particularly treasure is that in these days when most messages are prophecies of doom or hymns of negation (and in all these a note of welcome akin to rejoicing, all of which are the direst self-indulgence), O'Casey's music is inspired by a love of life. For all his curses, he is a yea-sayer. There is nothing abstract about his enthusiasm. He was cradled in the dank tenements of Dublin. His prose is salted by that working-class environment and refreshed by intimate contact with nature: wind, rain and the earth's flora.

What is even more important is that O'Casey's optimism—if one chooses to call it that—is rooted in, tested and fortified by a life of hardship, struggle and physical disability. We need such voices at present. Nothing is more mawkish and jejune than the 'futile fertilisers' who herald disaster. *Sunset and Evening Star*, the valedictory volume of O'Casey's life story, bears the following superb Chinese proverb as its epigraph: *'You cannot prevent the birds of sadness from flying over your head, but you can prevent them from building nests in your hair.'*

Additional Bibliography

The references in this list—arranged chronologically—comprise secondary material which may be of use in additional fields of biographical inquiry. They are mainly journalistic reports of topics of the day and controversies in which O'Casey became involved and was invited to comment. A brief annotation has been added where necessary.

'£200-a-Week Ex-Navvy Sees London: Motor Tour in a Cap and Dusty Clothes', *Daily Express* (London), 6 March, 1926, p. 9.

'Labourer Wins a Literary Prize: Mr O'Casey Eulogised by Lord Oxford', *Daily Express*, 24 March, 1926, p. 9.

Croft-Cooke, Rupert. 'The Real Sean O'Casey', *Theatre World* (London), October, 1926, p. 10.

'From Starvation to Success: The Dramatic Career of Sean O'Casey', *John O'London's Weekly* (London), 19 November, 1927, p. 200.

Lewis, Robert. 'Visiting Sean O'Casey in Devon: Informal Talks with Irish Playwright', *New York Herald Tribune*, 29 July, 1951, Section 4, p. 2.

Bellak, George. 'Tea With Sean', *Theatre Arts* (New York), **37** (September, 1953), pp. 70–1, 91–2.

'He Called O'Casey "Unsavoury"; Ex-Fun Fair Man Puts Foot in it', *Daily Worker* (London), 20 February, 1954, p. 3. [J. Carlton, Chingford Council's Entertainments Manager, objected to Chingford's Unity Theatre performing *Bedtime Story*.]

'New Play in Dublin', *Time* (New York), **65** (14 March, 1955), p. 74. [Review of *The Bishop's Bonfire*, plus O'Casey's comments to *Time* on the nature of his political faith.]

'O'Casey's Return to Irish Stage', *Daily Worker* (New York), 30 March, 1955, p. 7. [O'Casey's championship of freedom for the individual and hatred of oppression, as occasioned by the Dublin premiere of *The Bishop's Bonfire*.]

Gould, Jack. 'TV: Sean O'Casey is Interviewed; Irish Playwright Seen on N.B.C. Program', *New York Times*, 23 anuary, 1956, p. 49.

Hewes, Henry. 'Mirror in the Hallway', *Saturday Review of Literature* (New York), **39** (22 September, 1956), p. 30. [Visiting O'Casey in Torquay, on the occasion of the Broadway dramatisation of *Pictures in the Hallway*.]

'Personality Cult scorned by O'Casey. Author, in Phone Interview, Talks of Many Things—Working on a "Frolic" ', *New York Times*, 25 August, 1957, p. 112. [Provoked by the success of *Purple Dust* in New York, with plans later that year to stage *Cock-a-doodle Dandy*.]

O'Leary, Con. ' "Abbey Can't Have My Plays"—O'Casey', *Sunday Press* (Dublin), 27 July, 1958, p. 1. [Playwright's ban on all professional productions of his plays throughout Ireland after the withdrawal of *The Drums of Father Ned* from the Dublin Drama Festival earlier in the year.]

'Sean May End Ban on Abbey', *Sunday Review* (Dublin), 20 September, 1959, p. 28. [Speculation as to whether O'Casey would have a change of heart following a visit by Ernest Blythe to O'Casey in Torquay.]

'O'Casey May Let the Abbey Stage His Plays', *Sunday Press*, 20 September, 1959, p. 5.

'TV Show Drops O'Casey Interview', *Irish Times* (Dublin), 20 (15 March, 1960), p. 11. [Ed Sullivan programme cancelled excerpt of Barry Fitzgerald–O'Casey from the Abbey Theatre filmed documentary, *Cradle of Genius*, because of alleged hostility in America to the playwright as a true representative of Ireland.]

Funke, Lewis. '[Birthday] Interview', *New York Times*, 27 March, 1960, Section 2, p. 1.

Coogan, Beatrice. 'The Prophecy of Sean O'Casey', *Irish Digest* (Dublin), April, 1960, pp. 80–93.

'The Londoner's Diary: No Smooth Talk', *Evening Standard* (London), 22 July, 1961, p. 6. [Telephone comments from O'Casey on the eve of the London première of *The Bishop's Bonfire*.]

Gunn, John. ' "Telly? Count Me Out", says O'Casey', *Sunday Review*, 13 August, 1961, p. 28. [The playwright's ban on future TV productions of his plays.]

' "I Won't Write For Abbey"—O'Casey', *Sunday Press*, 4 March, 1962, p. 5.

Hennigan, Aidan. 'O'Casey Rejects Plea', *Irish Press* (Dublin), 20 March, 1962, p. 3. [Playwright's embargo on professional productions of his plays in Ireland not lifted.]

'O'Casey Gives Play to Telefis', *Sunday Press*, 24 June, 1962, p. 4. [Permission given by O'Casey in an interview with Edward Roth at Torquay for Telefis Eireann to broadcast *The Moon Shines on Kylenamoe*.]

'O'Casey Angry About Strike Call Now', *Irish Times*, 14 April, 1964, p. 1. [Abbey Players' threatened strike in support of a pay dispute, jeopardised their participation in the World Theatre season in London, but a settlement enabled the performances to go ahead as scheduled.]

Drummond, Angus. 'O'Casey Says', *Courier* (London), 42, no. 4 (April, 1964), pp. 40–1.

Scully, Seamus. ['Anecdotes'], *The World of Sean O'Casey* (London, 1966), pp. 181–4. [A Dubliner's recollections.]

Rodgers, W. R. 'A Good Word for Sean', *The Sunday Times* (London), 20 September, 1964, p. 15. [Obituary.]

Index

The titles of Sean O'Casey's works and projected works are indexed as a separate alphabetical sequence under O'Casey, Sean, *writings* – the last of seven such groups of sub-headings, the others being *summary estimates and impressions; biographical facts and facets; glimpses of, in various settings; physical traits; personal qualities and descriptive labels; literary qualities, attitudes etc.* Sub-entries within each of these groups are arranged in chronological or alphabetical order as appropriate.

O'Casey's views on people and topics are indexed, *in italic figures*, under the appropriate headings. Figures in **bold type** indicate an account or view of O'Casey.

and eyesight, 1, 7, 13, 20, 27, 37–8,
47–8, 52, 55, 56, 58, 60, 63, 75,
80, 83, 89, 99, 106; in last years,
128, 131, 134, 144, 146–9, 151,
161, 165, 169; speech, 3, 21, 30–32,
47, 48, 60, 63, 95, 108–15, 133,
151, 165, 171; reproductions of his
accent, 30–2, 108–15
*personal qualities and descriptive
labels*: argumentativeness and
pugnacity, 6, 57, 83, *132*, 151, 167;
an atheist, 145; bitterness (or its
absence), 4, 34–5, 72, 73, *129*, *136*,
140–1, *162*, 172; clowning, love of,
88, 146; a Communist, 72, *81*, *100*–
101, *108*, *142–3*, 155, 166;
compassion and concern for
humanity, 2, 15, 46, 99, 141, 151,
167; courage, 2, 5, 9–10, 132, 151;
egalitarian Irishism, 52; an exile
from everything, 103; exuberance,
4, 6; a Gaelic-speaker, 126, 157–8;
gentleness and kindness, 4, 5, 6,
41, 52, 72, 76, 132, 135, 141, 151,
167; a heretical humanist, 145;
integrity, 2; irascibility, *137*, 140–1,
152, 172; knowledge, width of,
169–70; laziness, *21*, 22, 82; life,
love and enjoyment of, *86*, *103*,
132, *134*, 145, *150*, 157, 159, 172;
mimicry, skill in, 4, 151; modesty
and dislike of publicity, 6, 29, 41,
132, 151, 169; optimism, 169, 173;
patience (or the reverse), 5, 60; a
Protestant, 99, 143, *168*; a religious
man, 81; restlessness, *85*;
sensitiveness, 15, 72; shyness (or
the reverse), 5, 72, 75, 151; song,
love of, 3, 4, 142, 144, 151, 158;
'sting and twinkle' duality, 2,
124–7, 128, 152, 169; tactlessness,
152, *154*; telephone, avoidance of,
40; tolerance, 80; a visionary
humanist, 158; a whiskey
teetotaller, 151
literary qualities, attitudes etc. (*see
also* playwrights; theatre): anti-
heroism, 84; autobiographies his
masterpiece, 167, 171;
characterisation, strength in, 17, 18;
characters not unattractive, *83–4*;
drawn from real life, *102*; 'copper
phrases' turned to gold, 62;

dialogue, thinking in, *105*;
dramatic technique and rules,
dislike of, 22, *44*, 55; dramatic
technique, pioneering achievements
in, 158; dramatist's view of life, *34*,
experience as basis, *22–3*, *23–4*, *54*;
fantasy and expressionism, 117–
118; journalists, all writers are,
126; lyricism, 171; naturalism, 34;
new subjects, need for, *58*; novel-
writing, disdain for, 22, 55; *plays*:
belittled, 99; neglected, 105; even
in Russia, 83; banned by O'C. in
Ireland, 106, 130, 132–3, 168;
early and late plays, 126; O'C.'s
favourites, conflicting statements
on, *48*, *94–5*, *102*, *129*, *137*, *162*;
reporter, O'C. a, 36; a slow writer,
49, 57; suggestions, amenability to,
43–4; thinking and planning
preferred to actual writing, 102;
working habits, 22, 57, 149,
159–60
writings: 'The Bald Primaqueera'
(1964), 159, 165; *The Bishop's
Bonfire* (1955), *81*–2, *84*, *137*, 167;
Gaiety production, 73, *118–19*;
Blasts and Benedictions (1967), 2,
5, 26, 64, 65–9, 105, 159, 165;
Cathleen Listens In (1923), 23;
Abbey production, 24–5, *51*; *Cock-
a-Doodle Dandy* (1949), 10, 26;
N.Y. production (1958), 89, 91;
O.C.'s favourite, *94–5*, *102*, *129*;
The Cock Crows (unwritten), 26;
Crimson in the Tri-colour (1921):
rejected by Abbey, 17, 18, 51; *The
Drums of Father Ned* (1960), *81*,
90, 94, 106, 107; Hornchurch
production, 108, 111–15; *Drums
Under the Windows* (1945), 72,
76; *Feathers from the Green Crow*
(1962), 1, 4, 13, 15, 50; *The Flying
Wasp* (1937), 2, 39, *109–10*; *The
Frost in the Flower* (1919):
rejected by Abbey, 17, 31, 45, 51,
165; *The Green Crow* (1956), 2;
reason for title, 95, 116; *The
Harvest Festival*: rejected by
Abbey, 17, 31, 45, 51; *I Knock at
the Door* (1939), 1, 44, 57, 89, 102,
132, 171; *Inishfallen, Fare Thee
Well* (1949), 5, *81*, 132; *Juno and*

O'Casey, Sean, *writings* (cont'd)
the Paycock (1924), 15, 34, 51;
O'C. compared to Joxer Daly, 4;
Abbey production, 17–18, 20, 36,
46, 75, 96–7, 165; London
production, 21, 23–32 *passim*,
40–1; belittled, 25, *43*, *48–9*, *57*,
105; Joxer Daly can be found
anywhere, *58*; attacked by Maud
Gonne, 71; quoted, 86, 121–2;
musical based on, 86–8; Abbey
Theatre Company production
(Aldwych, 1960), 135, 141; *letters*:
projected edition of, 1, 145, 150,
159, 169; to Susan Brown, 7–8; to
Saros Cowasjee, 102; to Lillian
Gish, 64; to Judy Goldberg, 8–9;
to Lady Gregory, 9; to John
O'Riordan, 132; to David
Phethean, 114–15; to O. Prudkov,
93; *The Moon Shines on
Kylenamoe* (1961), 26; *Pictures in
the Hallway* (1942), 1, 89, 132;
The Plough and the Stars (1926),
20, 25, *43*, 51, 84, 138, 148; Abbey
première, 23: Abbey disturbances,
25, 33–4, 70–1, 96, *112*; belittled,
105; Mermaid production, 127;
Aldwych production, 141; *Purple
Dust* (1940), *129–30*, 167; N.Y.
production, 56–7; Mermaid
production, 167; *The Red Lily*
(unwritten), 23–4, 26, 56–7; *Red
Roses for Me* (1942), 7, 73–5, 167;
Embassy production, 70, 72;
Mermaid production, 127; quoted,
136, 157; *Rose and Crown* (1952),
7, 39, 57; *The Shadow of a
Gunman* (1923), 15, 16, 20, 22, 31,
55, *91*, 165; Abbey production, 5,
35–6, 51; *The Signal* (unwritten),
26; *The Silver Tassie*, 27, *43–4*,
49, 56, *58*, 71–2, 158; Shaw on,
4–5; rejected by Abbey, 43, 45–6, –
162, *164*; O'C.'s favourite, *48*, *129*,
162; *The Star Turns Red* (1940),
101, 120; *The Story of the Irish
Citizen Army* (1919), 50; *Sunset
and Evening Star* (1954), 5, 80,
136, 173; *The Sword on the Cross*
(unwritten), 42; *Under a Colored
Cap* (1963), 2, 10, 129, 131, 132,
134–5, 143; *Windfalls* (1934), 44;

Withered Heather (*c.* 1897), 45;
Within the Gates (1933), 26, 37,
57; T. E. Lawrence on, 4; N.Y.
production, 5, 59–60, 63–4, 105,
169
O'Casey, Niall, 72, 85; death of, 79,
143, 146
O'Casey, Shivaun (Mrs Laurence
Kenig), 79, 85, 114–15, 144, 170
O'Connor, Frank: *Kings, Lords, and
Commons*, 120
O'Donnell, Frank Hugh, 71
O'Flaherty, Liam, *134*
Olivier, Sir Laurence, *130*
O'Neill, Eugene, 67, *68–9*, 85, *105*,
130
O'Neill, Maire (Molly), 97
O'Riordan, John, **1–10**, 132 **133–5**
Orwell, George, **6**
O'Toole National Club, *see* St
Lawrence O'Toole Club
Oxford University, 59, *103*

pacifism, *100*
Paler Shade of Green, A (Hickey and
Smith), 4, 35–6, 110
Pasternak, Boris: *Dr Zhigavo*, 93–4
Paul, St, *80*
Pearce, Patrick, 76
Penn, William, 56
Perrin, of Abbey Theatre, 17
Perth Repertory Club, 52
Pessimism, Theatre of, *165–6*
Phethean, David, **108–15**
Phillipson, Dom Wulstan, **75–7**
Picasso, Pablo, 81
Pinter, Harold, *159*
Plato: *The Republic*, 17
playwrights: necessary qualities of,
8–9, *134*, *159*; modern, diagnosed,
39–40, 44, 62, *65–9*, *134*;
Elizabethan and Restoration, *43*,
44, *69*
Plunkett, Jim, 161–2
poetry, need for in plays, *134*, *159*
policemen: English and Irish, 98
poverty, *136*; and the writer, *58*;
need to abolish, *100*
Prudkov, O., 93

Quinn, Tony, 16

radio, 56
Raphael, 17